TUFT THE WORLD

TUFT THE WORLD

An Illustrated Manual to Tufting Gorgeous Rugs, Decor, and More

TIERNAN ALEXANDER & TIM EADS

PA PRESS

PRINCETON ARCHITECTURAL PRESS · NEW YORK

Published by
Princeton Architectural Press
A division of Chronicle Books LLC
70 West 36th Street, New York, NY 10018
papress.com

27 26 25 24 4 3 2 1 First edition

Editor: Holly La Due
Designer: Natalie Snodgrass

Library of Congress Cataloging-in-Publication Data
Names: Alexander, Tiernan, author. | Eads, Tim, author.
Title: Tuft the world : an illustrated manual to tufting gorgeous rugs,
decor, and more / Tiernan Alexander and Tim Eads.
Description: First edition. | New York : Princeton Architectural Press,
[2024] | Includes bibliographical references. | Summary: "A celebration
of the craft of tufting rugs, home decor, and more that teaches the
basics about tufting machines, materials, and techniques; workspace
setup; and how to create projects from start to finish"
—Provided by publisher.
Identifiers: LCCN 2023027121 | ISBN 9781797224565 (paperback) |
ISBN 9781797227184 (ebook)
Subjects: LCSH: Rugs, Hooked. | House furnishings. | Tufting machines.
Classification: LCC TT850 .A3858 2024 | DDC 746.7/4—dc23/eng/20230725
LC record available at https://lccn.loc.gov/2023027121

Page 4: Sophie Bolton, *Wavy Rug*, machine-tufted cotton, hand stitched
Page 5: Molly Brennan, *Rug*, machine-tufted wool
Page 6: Molly Brennan, *Bikini Top*, machine-tufted wool
Opposite: Molly Brennan, *Bonnet*, machine-tufted wool, faux fur, satin ribbons
Cover: Juanita Salazar, *Wild Wild Vest*, vest and hat,
tufted and sewn acrylic, canvas, and felt (detail)

CONTENTS

Part One:
Craft

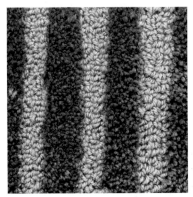

Part Two: Projects

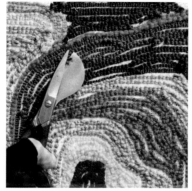

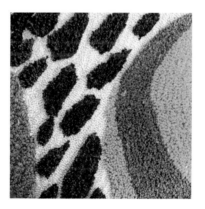

INTRODUCTION

ne of the best places I have had the good fortune to spend time in is the historic textile collection at the Winterthur Museum, Garden & Library in Wilmington, Delaware. As a graduate student in decorative arts and material culture, I was given access to drawers full of impossibly tiny embroidered baby pillows, an enormous storehouse with racks and racks of silk damask curtains or panels of sheer cotton voile, entire rooms full of carefully folded and boxed quilts. And rugs. From Persian silks to old cotton rags, the rugs were astounding. They told the stories of their times, their houses, their makers, and all the feet that had tracked mud over them or danced across their matted surfaces. Hearth rugs of wool (which is resistant to burning), tapestries to cover walls and curtain beds in warmth, and hand-knotted silk carpets brought by sea from around the world to dazzle and impress.

Somewhere lost in all that splendor, I became entranced with hand-sewn rugs from the American past. Rugs that were carefully designed and created primarily by women working at home to bring sophistication and color to their early nineteenth-century spaces. Many designs felt surprisingly modern, often geometric, with local flowers or animals winding around their borders. So many of them could have been made today, two hundred years later, and they would retain their vibrant and whimsically individual nature. I thought, "Someday, I'll set aside some time to learn to make one of my own." I loved the idea of every home being filled with unique motifs and styles that weren't just purchased, but that really reflected the individual makers.

As it happens, I have always loved crafting. Knitting, ceramics, sewing, and cooking have all been ways of being creative in my life.

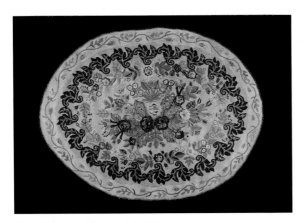

This vibrant oval floor mat depicts a bouquet of flowers and other plant life surrounded by three borders of leaves and vines. It was not made commercially but by an individual using wool yarn and a rug hook. It dates from 1825 to 1875 and was made in North America.

But I hadn't returned to the idea of rug making until recently. A few years ago, my partner, Tim, heard about machine tufting from a friend who worked at a rug-making company. He started trying to find a rug-tufting machine that he could play with. After some searching, he found a company in China willing to sell him one. Once he got one, he became obsessed. Unlike so many other crafts we had both tried, tufting was remarkably fast; he could make an area rug in an afternoon. He spent weeks experimenting with different yarns and cloth and built a half dozen frames before he perfected his tufting setup. He even made an ill-advised raid on the well-loved, and very pricey, stash of knitting yarn I'd collected over the years. The ensuing argument led to Tim's realization that he would need to find a more affordable (and less hazardous) source of tufting yarn.

Suddenly the ability was right there—not just for Tim and me, but for anyone to fill their home with colors and patterns without spending a month of Sundays sewing them by hand. Six years later, we have made more rugs than we can count and have traveled all over North America, teaching thousands of folks how to make rugs, pillows, and wall hangings galore. We have never had a student who couldn't make a rug. And we have been overwhelmed by the delight and creativity of rug makers of all skill levels.

As tufting has grown in popularity, classes have opened online in many cities and countries. Still, we wanted to write down all of the tufting experience and knowledge we learned through experimentation, collaboration, and time. Through a lot of classroom experience, we've come to realize that helping folks over the first few hurdles gives them the skills and confidence to create extraordinary artworks of their own. We've also tested numerous fabrics, yarns, glues, clippers, and more. This book represents all the tricks and tips we have accumulated and many inspirations from other artists along the way. We put all this together for anyone interested in getting started or improving their tufting skills.

This book will teach you to make a fantastic tufted rug of your design in just a few hours. So, what is tufting? Machine tufting is the process of pushing yarn through fabric to make a dense area of loops, or a fluffy field of cut yarn ends. As simple as it sounds, that

tuft (n.)
—

The Online Etymology Dictionary defines a tuft as a "bunch of soft and flexible things fixed at the base with the upper ends loose" from the late fourteenth century. Which is pretty accurate for our purposes. It is a word of uncertain origin, perhaps from the Old French *touffe*, which means "tuft of hair." Which, in turn, could be from the Latin *tufa*, "a kind of crest on a helmet." Or it could be derived from Old Norse *toppr*, "tuft or summit," which is where we get the word "top." Nevertheless, it has been used as a verb since the 1530s.

process is the basis for the majority of rugs and carpets you have walked on in your life. Unlike the sewn or woven rugs of the past, modern tufting made it possible to create vast expanses of carpet much more quickly and cheaply than ever before. And yet, for a hundred years, this has been primarily an industrial process using expensive machinery that only a few individuals had access to. The method of tufting has been invisible and unavailable to home crafters.

But that has changed suddenly in recent years. Tufting machines, cloth, frames, and myriad tools are now available for crafters world-wide, and this book is our guide to an endless world of tufted possibilities. From wall hangings and floor rugs to art pieces, clothing adornments, and decorative furnishings or gifts, *Tuft the World* will teach you to select the right tools, experiment with materials, create designs, and make quality tufted works. We've ruined so many rugs along the way, and while every failure has helped us grow as makers, it feels good to pass on the skills that will ensure that you can tuft beautiful and lasting objects.

Through this book, you can join a vibrant and growing community of tufters who are redefining the boundaries of the craft. People from all creative backgrounds, including those without experience, have been drawn to rug tufting in the past few years. Makers who have been into textile arts for a while—maybe working in embroidery, knitting, crocheting, or punch needle—will find that the tufting machine offers the opportunity to work more freely and at a larger scale. With a tufting machine, you can make bold designs faster and more spontaneously. It is like painting with yarn.

Tim working on *Curves and Waves*
and showing off his love of color.

WHAT YOU WILL FIND IN THIS BOOK
—

Part One, "Craft," covers the craft of tufting, with an illustrated overview of the tools, materials, and techniques needed to master rug making. You may already own a tufting machine or be in the market for one, so this part opens with a review of the types of machines you can use and what makes them different. In addition, we'll look at all the little accessories that make for a pleasant tufting experience, and we'll discuss which tools are must-haves and which are fun extras.

Setting up an adequate studio space—whether it is just a corner of your kitchen table or a whole room—calls for a few decisions about making or buying a tufting frame, what kinds of yarn and fabric you need, and what you'll want to have on hand so you can finish that first rug. You'll be introduced to the different types of tufting machines—cut, loop, combination, and high pile—and learn about their different qualities and how to operate them. We also included some information about color, design, and carving. The craft section closes with details on finishing rugs to make them last and some notes on troubleshooting common issues.

Part Two, "Projects," contains fifteen different tufting projects, from a simple mat to a multipart cat condo. Each project uses one of the different types of tufting machines, introduces new skills, or highlights a particular practice. After learning the basics in the first project, you can either go through the rest of the projects in order or jump around based on how you prefer to learn. The projects start with pieces for the floor and progress to wall hangings. Making wall work requires planning a hanging system that will keep the piece flat and support its weight, so we go over a few different options. The wall pieces also include ideas for adding macramé and mirrors as well as using cutting and carving for dimensional effects.

Almost everyone who starts tufting asks about how to wear their tufted pieces. Some simple recommendations about finishing will help your tufting be more flexible. We also include some ideas about using tufting as an embellishment for existing garments. Finally, the last few projects are about creating or covering three-dimensional objects. We explain how to create pattern pieces that can be tufted flat and assembled or sewn into objects, from cushions to chair covers. The projects include step-by-step instructions for users to follow but also serve as jumping-off points for more individual and elaborate creations of your own.

Scattered throughout this book you'll also find tales of tufting history we have collected. The development of rug making has included amazing inventions, cottage industries, and enterprising individuals whose ideas and artistry are still captivating today. And over the years, we've seen more pieces of stunning artwork in this field than we can recall. In many cases, these artists have inspired us to try more and to see new ways to use tufting as an art. So we've included images of various tufted art and features on different contemporary makers and their work. We hope these will introduce you to a vibrant community of tufters and provide inspiration for your projects.

And now—on to tufting!

opposite
Clutch, machine tufted with cut fabric strips, edged with twill tape and using folding brass hardware. Tassel made from wool.

Hand-Sewn Rugs in the United States

—

One of the most surprising things about homes before the industrial age is that the costliest home goods weren't the mahogany furniture or the silver tea set but the textiles. Curtains, bedcovers, and weavings were phenomenally expensive and thus were some of the biggest indicators of wealth. As a consequence, floor coverings were precious in the 1700s in North America. Most floors were wood or dirt and folks needed to be extremely wealthy to afford imported rugs simply to walk on.

When looking back at history, it can be easy to mischaracterize how objects were used due to our contemporary viewpoint. Because of their value, rugs in the period were used to cover beds and tables more often than floors. At one time, early American rugs were believed to be hearth covers or doormats made by women in their spare time out of fabric scraps to cover their bare floors. In fact, they were highly skilled forms of needlework that well-to-do girls learned to make in schools as a part of their formal education. These hand-sewn rugs have been mistaken for hooked rugs made from mass-produced designs popularized in the mid-1800s, more than one hundred years later. It's a little like confusing a 1970s' paint-by-numbers with an original oil painting made in 1850.

Yarn-sewn rugs were made by needle with a strand of two-ply yarn in a running stitch that left loops above the surface of a linen backing. They look very similar in technique to the tufted loop rugs or punch needle rugs of today. Far from being made of old yarn scraps, these were designed to be household art, made from new wool or silk. Another misconception about these rugs is that they were made to lie in front of the hearth to protect expensive imported rugs from sparks flying out of the fireplace. Since we know that yarn-sewn rugs were skillfully designed and produced, why did later generations assume they were only good for catching sparks or collecting mud? Probably because they no longer understood the great cost, skill, and meaning invested in each work.

In paintings of the era, there are depictions of lovely complex mats with floral and geometric designs lying in front of an empty fireplace in summer. This focal point in a parlor where guests were entertained was the perfect place to show off the handiwork of a skilled and creative daughter.

This nineteenth-century mat was hand sewn using wool dyed in vibrant colors. While many of the stripes have faded, the red and blue indicate the intensity of the other colors when new.

Craft

OVERVIEW

Making a tufted rug involves numerous components. This part of the book will help you get a handle on the tools and skills you can use to make any type of tufted piece.

Here is a brief overview of the tufting process, but all of these steps are discussed in detail later in this chapter. First, assemble your tools—a basic setup includes a tufting machine, frame, fabric, yarn, scissors, masking tape, markers, and threader (a paper clip will work). We'll talk about more complex setups a little later.

A tufting machine is your primary tool, followed by cloth and yarn. To tuft the yarn through the cloth, it must be stretched tightly over a wooden frame. Instructions on designing and building a frame are included in this chapter, but you can also buy a ready-made frame if you prefer. You can stabilize the frame by clamping it to a table or placing weights on the base if it is large enough to stand on the floor. When your frame is ready, stretch your fabric tightly across the carpet tack strip (see Tip, opposite), pulling it taut from top to bottom first, then side to side. Finally, use masking tape to cover the sharper areas of the frame.

After stretching the cloth, sketch your design with markers directly on the fabric. If you are making a detailed design, you can use a projector and trace the image. You always tuft from the wrong side of the finished piece, so your design will need to reverse how you want it to look when finished. Since you are working from the back, whatever you draw on the fabric will not show on the finished rug, so you can make as many adjustments or notes on the fabric as you wish.

With a design ready, you can pick your yarn colors. Most tufting uses two or three strands of yarn together at a time. Very thick yarn

TIP - Frames are made using carpet tack, which are thin strips of wood with hundreds of tacks sticking out from them on one side at an angle. These tacks are what hold your fabric in place while you are working. But be careful! Carpet tacks are supersharp, and most tufters initially cut themselves on them. Many folks take the extra precaution of using masking tape to cover the tacks while working.

Clockwise from top right: fabric shears, embroidery scissors, metal ruler, marker, thread snips, tufting machine, and assorted colors of wool yarn

may be used alone, but working with multiples makes a fuller effect more quickly. Using several strands of yarn at once also allows you to combine colors to make a mottled effect. Choosing and combining colors will be covered in the color section (see page 64).

Setting up the yarn correctly helps it flow smoothly into the machine as you work. A good yarn setup will include a place for your cones to stand and a yarn guide on your frame. You will feed the yarn through the guide and then thread it into your tufting gun. Once the machine is threaded, you push the needle into the fabric and tuft!

After you finish tufting, you will want to secure the yarn using carpet glue. Then you can add a backing cloth or bind the edges to create a finished piece.

That's the basic process from beginning to end.

Now that you have an overview, let's get into greater detail on what the different machines do, how to use them, and all the other elements of rug making from setup to finished masterpiece.

THE BASICS OF MACHINE TUFTING

**M**ost wall-to-wall carpets are produced on enormous looms with hundreds of needles working together to create carpets on long rolls. Handheld tufting machines are used in the rug industry as a supplemental tool for making detailed or intricate designs one needle at a time. They have also been used to make sample designs before putting something into industrial production. These handheld machines were expensive for the last half of the twentieth century and had been challenging to purchase individually. As a result, they have not been available for hobbyists and artists until recently.

But not all handheld tufting machines are the same. When selecting one for yourself, there are a couple of variations worth knowing about. All tufting machines vary in what type of pile they can make and how high that pile can be. The two types of pile are cut and loop. As a cut-pile machine pushes a loop of fabric into the backing, a scissor attachment or blade automatically cuts every loop; a loop machine leaves the surface uncut.

Left to right: The Duo, Loop, AK-III

Pile height is the length of yarn that extends above the backing material. The pile has to be long enough to thoroughly cover the backing material and it creates the cushion that determines how soft or luxurious it feels to walk on. A higher pile is fluffier and plusher, and extremely high pile (shag) carpet has gone in and out of fashion for decades.

The most common and least expensive tufting machines are low pile, ranging from 5 to 15 mm (less than ¼ to ½ inch). While that

Early Tufting Tools

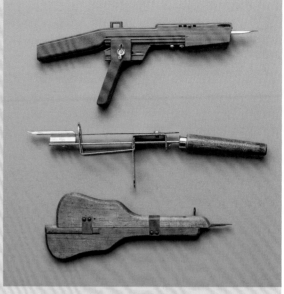

Tufting machines have their roots in rug hooking, an age-old craft that involves creating textiles by pulling loops of yarn or strips of fabric through a backing material. The basic mechanism of rug hooking is mirrored in tufting, where the same process of pushing material through an open-weave fabric is employed. The earliest tufting machines were simple wood-and-metal tools that date back to the mid- to late 1800s. One of the most famous examples is the Susan Burr machine (sold as Ye "Susan Burr" Hooked Rug Machine), which is still available for purchase on online platforms such as eBay.

Top to bottom: two early speed tufting tools; Ye "Susan Burr" Hooked Rug Machine

High-pile sample with metal ruler

is a pretty small difference, that variation can create stunning visual effects. These machines are lightweight and come in three types: cut only, loop only, or combination cut and loop. Combination machines were initially much more expensive, but the technology keeps getting better, and they are now available at a similar price to the cut or loop only machines.

In addition to the three low-pile machines described above, there is a fourth type, often called an industrial or pneumatic machine. Industrial machines can make pile heights ranging from 20 to 60 mm (¾ to 2½ inches). It uses forced air to push the strands of yarn out to such great lengths. This machine can make the shaggiest of shag carpets and can be converted from cut to loop. They tend to cost about three to five times as much as the low-pile machines, and to have the forced air they require the purchase of an air compressor.

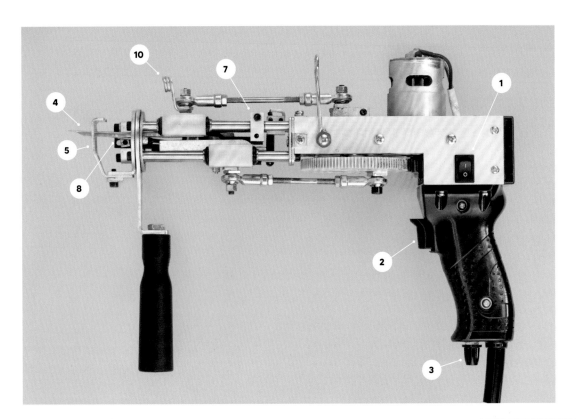

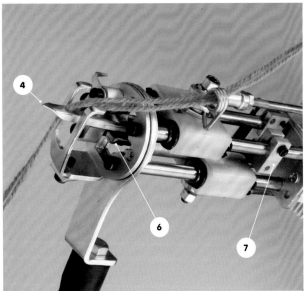

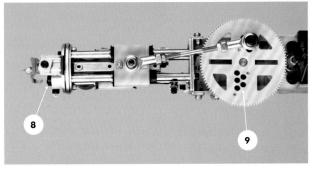

The major parts of the low-pile cut-and-loop (The Duo) tufting machine:

1. Power switch
2. Trigger
3. Speed control
4. Needle
5. Foot
6. Cloth pusher
7. Scissor opener
8. Scissor closer
9. Pile height holes
10. Threading loop

The Future of Tufting Machines
—

The most requested item from tufters is a machine that can tuft high pile without needing a compressor. There are a couple of machines in development now that will be able to tuft medium pile (20 to 30 mm) or high pile (35 to 45 mm). Current low-pile machines tuft from 7 to 18 mm.

The new medium- and high-pile machines won't need a compressor and will be comparable in price to low-pile machines. The AK-III will still have a place as a more powerful industrial machine that can tuft a much wider range of heights, But this change will make dimensional tufting much more accessible.

GETTING TO KNOW YOUR MACHINE
—

Now, let's look at how our tufting machine (also called a tufting gun) works. The machine we will use most in the book is a combination cut-and-loop low-pile tufting machine sold as the Duo. It has a small pair of scissors that snip the yarn after each stitch to create a cut pile. You can also disengage the scissors and let every stitch stay connected as a string of loops.

Like most tufting machines, the Duo has a two-handle construction with a needle (#4) and foot (#5), as seen in the top image on page 28. When the machine is pressed against the tightly stretched fabric, the needle pokes through to the other side, while the foot stays pressed against the fabric, guiding the movement of the needle. This creates an entry for the yarn, like a needle does in a sewing machine. But unlike a sewing machine, where you move the fabric and the machine stays still, in this case, you drive the machine around on the fabric. The knob under the handle (#3 on the machine opposite) allows you to adjust the tufting speed.

TUFTING
—

One of the most important things about the tufting process is learning how much pressure to use when pushing the machine into the cloth. The foot of the machine must always stay in contact with the cloth, so you're putting a significant amount of pressure on the cloth. Not enough pressure will cause the machine to bounce off the

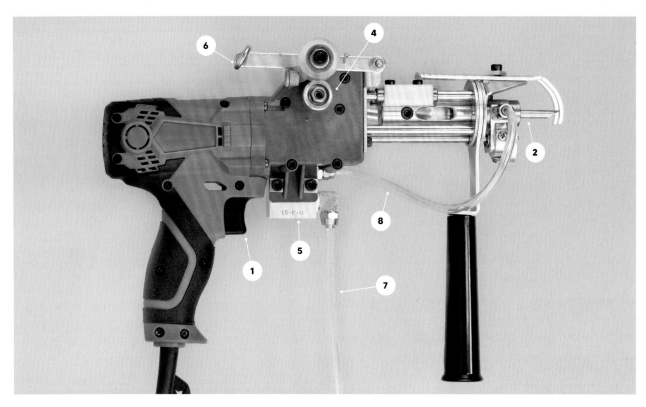

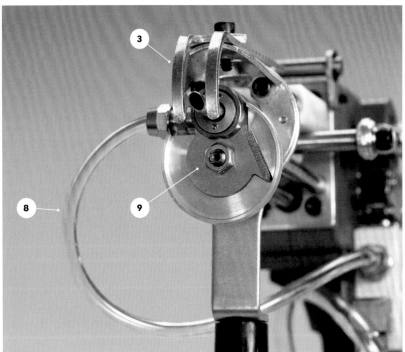

The major parts of the high-pile pneumatic (AK-III) tufting machine:

1. Trigger
2. Needle
3. Foot
4. Feed wheel
5. Air valve
6. Threading loop
7. Hose to air compressor
8. Hose to needle
9. Cutting blade

 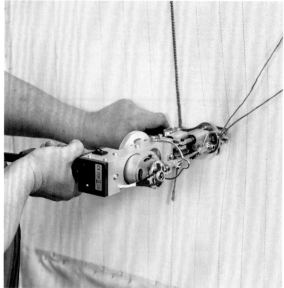

above left
This machine is too far away from the fabric, which is causing issues with tufting. The machine should be pushed fully against the fabric, hard enough to create a depression in the surface.

above right
Tim is holding the machine on its side in order to tuft a line from left to right.

cloth and not push the yarn into the backing. This is why stretching the fabric tight on the frame is critical and why the frame must be clamped to a sturdy table.

Tufting machines are made to only move in one direction. Just as you can't make a car move sideways but instead have to turn the front wheels to lead the whole car into a turn, the tufting machine always wants to move a certain way and can't be pulled sideways. When held upright, it will naturally move up the cloth. If you want to tuft a line from left to right, you have to turn the whole machine so the top is now facing the right, as shown above right. If you are holding the machine upright, you can push into the fabric near the bottom of the frame and tuft a line of stitches going straight up from the bottom to the top of the frame with no turns to the left or right. To go down, you have to rotate the machine until it is fully upside down, so the needle and foot are oriented correctly against the cloth. If you don't rotate the machine while changing direction, you will shred the cloth.

As you become comfortable orienting your machine to the tufting, you can continue to tuft by driving the machine in different directions. Or you may prefer to fill in designs by starting at the bottom and tufting upward, moving the machine back to the bottom and tufting another line next to the first until the design is filled in. These techniques will be used in the projects in this book so that you can try them out.

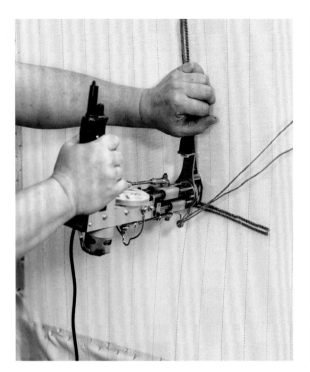

These two images show the right and wrong way to make a line of tufting from the top of the frame to the bottom.

On the left, Tim is holding the machine upside down, so it will easily tuft downward. In the image on the right, the machine is held upright while being dragged downward. This is causing the machine to shred the fabric instead of tufting a row.

MAKING ADJUSTMENTS
—

As you tuft, practice with the machine settings to integrate different effects into your work, such as pile height, speed, yarn tension, and stitch type. These variations exist on most machines, although there might be differences in the mechanics. Changing from cut to loop is very different on the industrial machines since they have a much more extensive range of pile height. But otherwise, these are pretty universal variations.

Now that you have a basic working knowledge of your tufting machine, we can look at how to set up your workspace.

MAKING SPACE

Spaces for tufting vary widely depending on the size of work you make and the amount of space you can dedicate. Whether compactly laid out on a kitchen table or decking out a full room, this section will go over the necessities and possibilities for your workspace. The primary element of your tufting space is the frame. We'll start with making a tufting frame based on available space and how to secure the frame to a table or the floor.

You will also have a selection of yarn, tufting and backing fabrics, one or more tufting machines, and a bunch of working and finishing tools like scissors, weights, rulers, and glue. A simple setup can be made with two or three storage bins and a small frame that can be stashed under a bed or in a closet. You want to take care when storing your machine as it can catch on fabric and get tangled in yarn or damaged if knocked around. Keep it in its original case, a storage box, or wrapped loosely in packing material like perforated cardboard to protect the needle tip and power switch. Flip-top bins that stack well and hold substantial amounts of yarn and cloth are also great for keeping your tufting supplies out of sight.

If you tuft often, there are several ways to keep everything out in the open and ready to use. Our studio includes a set of shallow shelves for cones of yarn, pegboards to hang tools on, and a large worktable that can hold a tabletop frame as well as being a great space for carving, trimming, or finishing.

We installed French cleats along one wall to create a versatile system for both storage and displaying art. French cleats are an art hanging system that will be featured on some of the wall-hanging projects. It is a two-part hanger where one piece is mounted to the wall and the other is attached to the back of what you want to hang.

By installing rows of wood wall cleats, anything with a hanging cleat on the back can be positioned anywhere along the wall. This modular system makes it easy to temporarily transform a living space into a working studio.

If you have the space, a freestanding tufting frame is another great piece of equipment. Now let's move on to making and setting up the frame.

MAKING A FRAME
—

All machine-tufted rugs must be made on a frame. The frame holds up the primary tufting cloth so that you can work into it, like an easel holds up a canvas for painting. Frames can be made in any size, but they are mostly divided into ones that are small enough to clamp to the top of a table or so large that they stand on the floor. Tabletop frames tend to be around a square yard or meter, while freestanding frames can be as large as your space allows. You can purchase a premade tufting frame online and assemble it yourself. These are usually small enough to clamp to a tabletop and are great for getting started quickly since they can usually be set up in less than twenty minutes with some basic tools. Many will require clamps to secure them, but they aren't usually sold together, so make sure to buy a pair that will accommodate your worktable.

Carpet tack is widely available at home improvement stores. It is a thin strip of wood with hundreds of very sharp tack ends sticking out from it at an angle. Tufting frames use carpet tack to hold the fabric on the frame because it allows users to adjust and reposition the cloth as needed. It can also withstand the pull of the fabric as it is stretched and worked. Since it is so sharp, it's good to wear thick work gloves when assembling the frame to avoid any cuts.

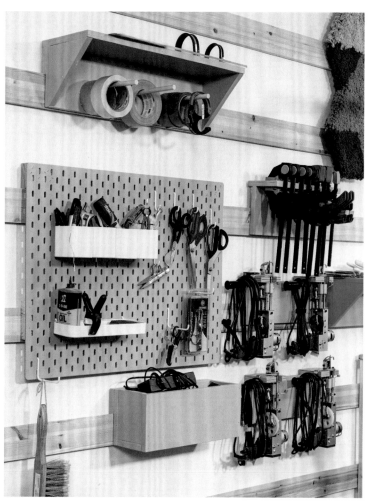

above

Every pine board on the wall is one half of a French cleat. And each of the blue objects hanging there has the opposite piece of the cleat attached to its back.

left

The wooden board attached to the wall has been cut along the upper edge at a 45-degree angle, making a small, triangular space between the board and wall.

TABLETOP FRAME

– – – –

FINISHED SIZE: 30 × 30 inches (76.2 × 76.2 cm)

MATERIALS:

1. Work gloves
2. 1 pine board, 1 × 4 × 34 inches (2.5 × 10.2 × 86.4 cm)
3. 2 pine boards, 1 × 4 × 30 inches (2.5 × 10.2 × 76.2 cm) each
4. 2½-inch (6.4 cm) wood screws
5. Screwdriver, electric drill, or impact driver
6. 1 pine board, 1 × 4 × 29¼ inches (2.5 × 10.2 × 74.3 cm)
7. 4 pieces carpet tack, 30 inches (76.2 cm) each
8. Wood glue
9. Hammer or pneumatic stapler
10. 1-inch (2.5 cm) nails or staples
11. 2 pine boards, 1 × 4 × 12 inches (2.5 × 10.2 × 30.5 cm) each
12. Eye screws
13. ½-inch (1.2 cm) drill bit (Forstner is preferred, but any bit will work)
14. 2 dowel rods, 6 inches (15.2 cm) long, ½ inch (1.2 cm) diameter
15. 2 clamps (sized for your worktable)

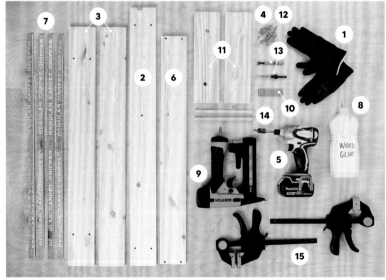

Lay out the four boards that make up your frame. Start with the 34-inch (86.4 cm) board, which will be the base. Place the two 30-inch (76.2 cm) side boards on the base 2 inches (5 cm) from the ends and attach them with the wood screws. [**FIG.1**] The end pieces are where the clamps will hold the frame to the table. In this example, we've predrilled our holes to keep the wood boards from splitting.

—

Flip your frame over and attach the 29¼-inch (74.3 cm) top board to the two sides using the wood screws. [**FIG.2**]

—

Lay out the carpet tack so it matches the boards. The top and sides will be completely covered in tack, and the base will have tack between the two ends that extend past the sides. The tack will be attached with both glue and nails for extra strength.

—

Run a thin line of glue along the narrow edge of each board and along the smooth side of the tack. When attaching the tack to the bottom board, leave the ends past the side boards without carpet tack. Make sure the tacks all point away from the center on all sides. [**FIG.3**] See detail image on page 45, Fig 5.

—

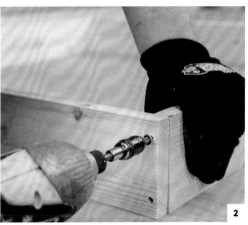

TIP - Each tack on the wooden strip is angled to one side of the board like a row of eyelashes. For the fabric to grip onto them, they need to point away from the center of the tufting area. So, at the top of the frame the tacks should point upward, at the bottom they point down, on the right side they should bend to the right, etc.

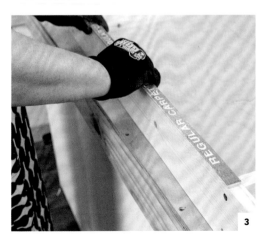

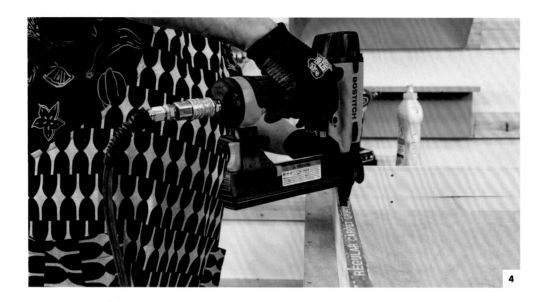

4

Hammer or staple the tack to each board using 4 or 5 nails or staples per piece. [**FIG. 4**]

—

Assemble the yarn holder and feeder. Make two marks on one 12-inch (30.5 cm) board 3 inches (7.6 cm) in from each end; this will be the yarn holder. The marks should also be centered on the width of the board.

—

The other 12-inch (30.5 cm) board will be the yarn feeder, and it will be attached above the yarn holder. Mark a spot on the edge of the feeder board above the mark you just made on the yarn holder board. This is where you will attach the eye screws.

—

Attach the two eye screws. [**FIG. 5**]

—

With the Forstner drill bit, drill a ½-inch (1.2 cm) circle into the holder board, being careful not to go through to the other side. These holes will hold your dowel rods. [**FIG. 6**]

—

Attach the holder and feeder boards to the right or left side of your frame, depending on what your dominant hand is. In our case we are making this frame for a right-handed person, so we will be attaching them to the right side of the frame.

—

To correctly place the holder and feeder, mark the side of your frame 4 inches (10.2 cm) from the top for the feeder board and again 4 inches (10.2 cm) from the bottom for the holder.

—

Predrill two holes in the side of the frame for both the holder and the feeder, and then drill matching holes into the ends of the boards. You can also use L brackets if that's easier.

—

Attach the yarn holder and feeder boards to the frame. [**FIG. 7**]

—

Install the dowel rods. Clamp to the table.

Larger frames are made of thicker wood (2 × 4 inches/5 × 10.2 cm) since they have to hold up more weight and need more structural integrity. Since this frame will stand on the floor, it will need braced legs to distribute the weight and create stability. In addition to the legs and feet, it is best to secure the frame to the floor since tufting involves putting a lot of pressure on the frame. Sandbags laid over the feet will hold the frame in place, and they can usually be found at a hardware or garden supply store. It is best to use one bag on each side; 20 pounds (9 kg) each should be enough weight.

Another way to stabilize a large frame is to rest some of the weight against a wall. When the frame is complete, you can add boards to the top that will touch the wall, keeping everything balanced.

Tufting cloth length (157 inches/4 m width)	Frame size	Yield of tufted pieces
1 yard (91 cm)	30 × 30 inches (76 × 76 cm)	4
	48 × 30 inches (122 × 76 cm)	3
2 yards (182 cm)	66 × 30 inches (167 × 76 cm)	4
	66 × 44 inches (167 × 111 cm)	3
	66 × 72 inches (167 × 183 cm)	2
3 yards (274 cm)	96 × 44 inches (244 × 111 cm)	3
	96 × 72 inches (244 × 183 cm)	2

This table indicates how many rugs you can get out of a piece of tufting cloth based on the size of your frame.

When making larger frames, you need to use the board's strength to keep it from warping. A long, narrow plank will flex along one orientation but not along the other. To take advantage of this, the larger frame will have the wider side facing forward rather than the edge. This will create a much more robust frame and prevent it from bending when you stretch your cloth.

When working on a larger frame, you can build a freestanding yarn holder or one integrated with the frame. In both scenarios, it helps to have feeder loops attached near the top of the frame. Having the yarn feed down from above always makes for the smoothest flow of yarn to the machine and prevents tangles. Yarn holders also keep the yarn moving without the cone of yarn getting tipped over or rolling away.

We recommend making your frame based on the size of tufting cloth you can get. The frame sizes in the chart are based on white primary tufting cloth that is 157 inches (4 m) wide. If you stick to the frame sizes in the chart, you will have little to no waste with that size of tufting cloth.

FREESTANDING FRAME

_ _ _ _

FINISHED SIZE: 72 × 66 inches (196 × 168 cm)

MATERIALS:

1. Work gloves
2. 2 pine boards, 2 × 4 × 66 inches (5 × 10 × 168 cm), for frame
3. 2 pine boards, 2 × 4 × 72 inches (5 × 10 × 183 cm), for frame
4. Screwdriver, electric drill, or impact driver
5. 5-inch (13 cm) wood screws
6. 3-inch (7.5 cm) wood screws
7. 4 L brackets
8. Carpet tack, enough to cover 276 inches (701 cm) in length
9. Wood glue
10. Hammer or pneumatic stapler
11. 1-inch (2.5 cm) nails or staples
12. 4 pine boards, 2 × 4 × 24 inches (5 × 10 × 61 cm), for legs and feet
13. 4 pine boards, 2 × 4 × 11 inches (5 × 10 × 28 cm) with 45-degree miter cut, for leg supports
14. 3 pine boards, 2 × 4 × 16 inches (5 × 10 × 41 cm), for yarn holder and feeder
15. ½-inch (1 cm) round bit; Forstner is preferred, but any bit will work
16. 2 dowel rods, 6 inches (15.2 cm) long, ½ inch (1.2 cm) diameter
17. Eye screws
18. Sandbags

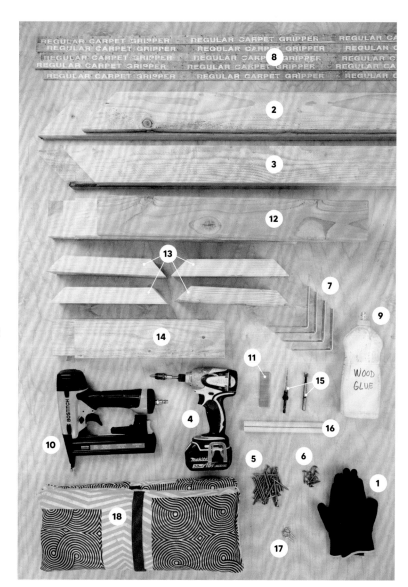

A completed large frame including
yarn holder, wall brackets, and
weighted bags over the feet.

Lay out the boards for the frame on the floor of your workspace or on a large table and separate them by size. The two 66-inch (168 cm) pieces are for the vertical portion of the frame, while the 72-inch (183 cm) pieces will be the horizontal top and base.

—

Screw the frame boards together to create a large rectangle using the 5-inch (13 cm) wood screws. [**FIG.1**]

—

Using the shorter (3-inch/7.5 cm) screws, attach an L bracket in each corner to give your frame extra stability. [**FIG.2**]

—

Next, attach the carpet tack to the front edge of the wide part of the board. It is important to remember that the tacks will all need to angle away from the center of the frame. The tack will first be glued to the boards and then nailed or stapled into place for extra strength.

—

Run a thin line of glue along the edge of each board and along the smooth side of the tack. The tack will cover the edges of the top and bottom pieces from end to end. It will cover the side boards from the top to the frame base, stopping short of the legs. [**FIG. 3**]

—

Hammer or staple the tack to each board every 4 to 5 inches (10 or 12 cm.) [**FIGS. 4-5**]

—

Now it's time to create your legs and feet for your frame. Lay out the two 24-inch (61 cm) pieces of lumber perpendicular to each other, then add the smaller mitered pieces for support. [**FIG. 6**]

—

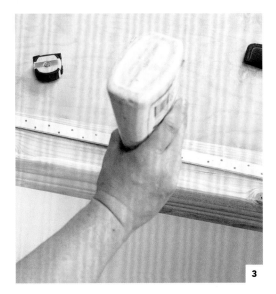

3

4

5

Screw the longer pieces together using 3-inch (7.5 cm) screws, then the mitered supports to tie the two perpendicular pieces together. Repeat this process for both legs. [**FIG. 7**]

—

It's time to attach the legs to the frame. Turn over the frame so you can attach the legs to the back side (the side opposite the carpet tack). The feet are parallel to the floor and give your frame stability. They attach to the end of the vertical boards with 3-inch (7.5 cm) screws.

—

6

For placement, measure 12 inches (30.5 cm) from the bottom of the frame on both sides and attach with 3-inch (7.5 cm) screws. When attaching, make sure each leg is parallel to the frame so that its foot will sit flat on the floor. [**FIG. 8**]

—

Assemble the yarn holder. The holder board will attach to the same side of the frame as the feeder board. These two items should be on the same side as your dominant hand. Make two marks on the board 3 inches (7.5 cm) in from the ends in the center of the width as shown in the project for a tabletop frame. Using a ½-inch (1 cm) round bit, drill out a circle of the board, being careful not to go through to the other side. This hole will be the right size to fit your dowel rods into. Insert the dowel rods into the holes.

—

Attach the feeder to the top back of the frame. Use the location of the dowels on the yarn holder below as a guide as to where to attach the eye screws. [**FIG. 9**]

—

Secure frame to the floor with weights or screws.

10

Test the strength of the frame once you have finished it. Take two steps away from the frame and lean against it. It should support your body weight without flexing much. If it bends out of shape or starts straining, we recommend adding wall supports to the top of the frame. This consists of adding two extra boards the length of half the frame foot plus the width of your frame, which is 14½ inches (36.8 cm), to the top of the frame, which will rest against the wall. Attach at the top right and left of your frame, protruding out the back (perpendicular to the frame). [**FIG. 10**]

Now the frame will be supported at the bottom (by the feet) and the top (by the newly attached boards). No amount of pressure against the frame will cause it to flex because the force is now being transferred to the wall of your workspace. (If you have thick molding or baseboards where the floor meets the wall, the top braces might need to be an inch or longer than the feet.)

Catherine Evans Whitener

In 1892, at the age of twelve, Catherine Evans attended a cousin's wedding where she saw a colonial-era candlewick bedspread given to the bride as a family heirloom. Fascinated, she wanted to make one like it, but couldn't find anyone who still knew the old technique. For several years she experimented with different embroidery stitches in hopes of producing something like it.

By fifteen, she had invented a style of work she called "turfing" because it looked like grass turf to her. She started by sewing a long running stitch of yarn into cotton cloth. She then pulled loops of the yarn up through the surface of the fabric, making designs with the loops. After it was finished, she boiled the fabric twice to make it shrink, which tightened the weave around the yarn and locked the design in place. She would then cut the loops to form tufted designs. These tufted textiles were called chenille, after the French word for caterpillar.

That year Catherine made a chenille bed-spread for her brother as a wedding present. People all over town wanted one like it, and within a year, she was making and selling bedspreads to other folks in her community in Dalton, Georgia. Soon she started teaching tufting to other girls and women so they could earn money for their families. Two years later, the demand for her tufted spreads was so steady that Catherine started the Evans Manufacturing Company with her brother. They would distribute supplies and patterns to families around the area to make the fabric and then drive around collecting the finished bedspreads from these "spread houses." The chenille fabric was so popular that it was made into robes, dresses, pillows, and other home goods sold all over the country.

Others in the region also capitalized on the boom in bedspreads and tufted textiles. Glenn Looper was a tufting entrepreneur who modified the Singer 31-15 industrial sewing machine to handle thicker yarn. Other inventors literally hacked off the front of a sewing machine and added multiple needles so it could tuft many rows at a time, thereby increasing the production speed. These machines were also perfect for making bath mats and small rugs. Around the same time, Looper also developed a motorized punch needle to speed up the hand tufting process. Further development of the tool by Joe McCutchen was used to grow his factory from forty machines in 1937 to four hundred, with 950 employees by 1939.

All of these developments grew out of a community that had taken to tufting so thoroughly that Dalton grew over the years to become the carpet-making capital of the world. And it all started with a young woman with great ideas and a desire to share them. Catherine Evans Whitener didn't make millions from her business—better than that, she created a hometown industry that still produces more than 80 percent of U.S. carpets and 45 percent of the world's.

above
Catherine Evans Whitener with one of her famous chenille bedspreads

left
Chenille bedspread with peacock

ADVANCED SETUP

—

You can tuft any style of rug or design with a basic tufting machine, but if you want to work with longer loops or deeper shag carpets, you can upgrade to an industrial tufting machine. Industrial or pneumatic machines use forced air to push longer sections of yarn through the needle, allowing for a greater variety of pile heights.

The AK-III Industrial Tufting Machine is both electric and pneumatic, meaning it must plug into the wall and connect to an air compressor to operate. Other examples of industrial machines are the Hofmann VML-16 and the ZQ-III, which also use compressors. Each of these machines comes with a small air hose incorporated into it, but they do not come with a compressor.

Tufting requires the type of air compressor that is compatible with spray guns or sanders and has an output of between five and seven cubic feet per minute (CFM) at 90 pounds per square inch (psi.) Air compressors that have a CFM lower than five at 90 psi will not supply enough air to support tufting.

For metric users, pounds per square inch is measured in kilopascals (kPa) or bars. Ninety psi is approximately 6.2 bars or 620 kilopascals.

Although tufting machines are a unique tool, they hook up to air compressors in the same way all air-driven tools do. Your local hardware store, auto parts store, or air compressor specialist will be able to help you purchase exactly what you need.

Because each country specifies different hose connections, it's hard to detail which precise fitting you might need. The manufacturer of the air compressor you purchase can advise you on which fittings will connect to your machine.

You also need to add a filter to the air compressor to prevent water from building up in the valve of the machine (especially if you live in a humid area). Without an added filter, water will eventually start to leak from the needle, causing serious damage to the air valve. Filters can be added anywhere between the compressor and the machine, but we recommend installing them where the compressor meets the machine's air hose, so it doesn't add more weight to the tufting machine itself. Make sure the fittings on your filter are compatible with the fittings on your hose.

Obviously, upgrading your setup to include an air compressor is a big commitment. But it does allow for a greater variety of tufted surfaces. If you are considering getting a compressor, it's good to know how loud it can be. There are ultraquiet models, but even with those, it can be a good idea to use ear protection. Industrial tufting guns are also heavier than regular machines and using one for hours can be quite the workout.

OPTIONAL TOOLS
—

We didn't want to end this chapter without mentioning some of the helpful and fun tools and materials that we also use often in our practice. Some of these will be discussed in greater depth in the next section or in specific projects. Each can help solve problems or just make your work a little easier.

Gloves
Any repetitive motion can cause irritation over time, and if you have carpal tunnel, it is important to protect your hands and wrists from further stress. Cycling gloves with pads in the palm can help protect your hand, wrist, and even arm and shoulder. The pads in the palm help absorb some of the pulsing of the machine, resulting in less stress on your joints.

Dust Mask or Respirator
Tufting with a cut-pile machine releases tiny bits of fibers into the air all the time. You will first notice this in the dust that settles on your frame and the floor around your workspace. It is never a good idea to inhale particles into your lungs, so we recommend working in a well-ventilated area or wearing a mask. Dust masks, like those used by woodworkers, are great at filtering particles out of the air you inhale. I prefer a half-face respirator since I can also use it when working with adhesives or other chemicals as there are filters that can capture both.

Air Scrubber or Filters
For long tufting sessions, we have an industrial air scrubber (a fancy way of saying a large filtration machine). It runs the entire time we are tufting to suck the fibers out of the air, and the filters are replaceable. You can also build an air scrubber using a box fan, a wooden box, and a few air filters. YouTube has some great videos on how to make these. If you don't plan to have an air scrubber, you can check the air filters in your home heating and air conditioning and consider changing them more often.

Scissors

It's nice to have a variety of scissors in your toolbox for different applications. Oversize scissors work well for cutting fabric, and duckbill or bent handle scissors are perfect for trimming rugs by hand. Embroidery scissors are suitable for minor touch-ups and for carving details into your piece. It is also lovely to have a scissor sharpener.

Shears

Several electric cutting tools at different price points can help clean up your finished rugs or add a carved dimension to your work. The main three are sheep shears, carving clippers, and electric scissors. Sheep shears and a shearing guide will allow you to shave your carpet to a perfectly level surface. Carving clippers are similar to hair clippers or pet clippers; they come with guards to keep you from cutting too deeply and can be used to create relief carving effects. Electric scissors are the most detailed carving tools, allowing for the most complex designs of the three.

left to right:
Fabric shears, bent handle scissors, bent handle carving scissors, embroidery (top), thread snips (bottom), sheep shears with guide, electric clippers, electric carving scissors

1. Felt
2. Woven
3. Nonskid, rubberized
4. Mesh
5. Nonskid, dots

Glue

Several different types of glue can be used in rug finishing. To glue the rug and lock in your tufts, we recommend a high-quality carpet adhesive for pieces on the floor. This is a glue that will withstand the hard use of floor rugs. You can use craft glue or PVA (polyvinyl acetate) glue for wall pieces or decorative work. After you glue up the back of the rug, you might want to add a backing material or edging tape. If the glue has already dried, you can use a spray adhesive to add fabric or a hot glue gun to add twill tape.

Glue Spreaders or Trowels

Many sizes of plaster or concrete smoothing trowels can be found at any hardware store. These are great for applying backing glue since they are helpful in scraping off the excess. This will save you money on glue and keep the rug from getting any hard lumps of glue.

Backing Cloth

After your rug is glued up, it can be hung on a wall or used as it is. But a nice finishing touch is to add a cloth backing. There are several kinds to choose from, including felt, woven, mesh, and nonskid. Each type of cloth serves a different purpose and is used for various applications. If you plan to glue or tack the rug down on the floor or to use it in an application like stair treads, mesh is best since it doesn't add bulk but provides a structure for gluing to another surface.

Any woven cloth can be used as backing, but you will want to find a way to finish the edges so they don't fray. You can fold the edges of the fabric when gluing if the rug isn't going to be too heavily used. For a stronger finish, use an edging like twill tape on top of the fabric, or you can have the edges professionally finished. Most major cities have a carpet-repair business that can serge or wrap the carpet edges. A solid professional finish will last a very long time and add to the look of your rug.

Felt is a great choice if you don't have access to professional carpet sergers and finishers; because it's a nonwoven fabric, it won't fray at the edges.

You can glue it on and trim it back to the edge of the rug, so it isn't visible from the front. And finally, nonskid works well on hardwood or tile floors where the rug or mat might slip out from under someone.

Tools

We have a small toolbox just for adjusting our machines. Our tools include an adjustable wrench, two sets of hex keys (SAE and metric), fine-point needle-nose pliers, and a screwdriver.

YARN, COLOR, AND DESIGN

ALL ABOUT YARN
—

Rugs are made from yarns of numerous materials and thicknesses. This section will discuss the best yarns and fabrics for tufting machines, how to adapt thinner fibers, and which yarns work best with which techniques. There are guidelines for what makes a great rug yarn, but to get into that, we will want to look at the yarn world overall. In addition to yarn, some folks enjoy experimenting with other fabrics, including used or dead stock cloth cut into strips. Once you have a good idea of the thickness needed to tuft and what will cut easily, you can try out any number of materials.

YARN WEIGHT
—

Although yarn is classified into "weights," we don't organize it according to its actual scale weight, such as ounces, grams, or pounds. Instead, the term "yarn weight" refers to the thickness of a single strand of yarn.

A yarn's weight is determined by measuring a strand's diameter—or the thickness. Holding a piece of string to a ruler to measure is pretty tough unless you have a great ruler and perfect vision. An easier way to talk about thickness is using the wrapping method.

Wrapping measures the yarn by taking a strand and wrapping it around a ruler until one inch (or one centimeter if you are counting wraps per centimeter) is covered. The number of yarn wraps in one inch is the wraps per inch or WPI. The higher the WPI, the thinner the yarn; the smaller the number, the chunkier the yarn.

Another system for measuring thickness was introduced by the Craft Yarn Council. The CYC standard yarn weight system has seven

Sample Books

—

Step back in time to the 1930s, when you were a yarn dyer on a mission to showcase your newest hues to the world. But wait, there's a catch—the internet's not a thing yet, and printing out colors just won't cut it. How do you show off the rich quality and vibrant variety of your yarns? Enter the magical world of yarn sample books! These were so ubiquitous that shelves would overflow with them and they would be discarded at the end of the season, or year. Some survive to this day like this one pictured from Winterthur.

different categories, numbered from 0 to 7. In this system, lower numbers indicate thinner yarn; the different yarn weights also have names, which are often used on yarn labels. The categories are (from 0 to 7): lace, super fine, fine, light, medium, bulky, super bulky, and jumbo.

"Ply" refers to how many strands are twisted together to make up a yarn. If you look at a single length of yarn and it appears like there are two or three strands twisted together, that yarn is either two- or three-ply. Notably, the measure of thickness refers to the whole yarn, not the individual plies. The reason for plying yarn is that it is typically much stronger than single ply even at the same thickness. Where it can be easy to pull one ply of yarn or thread apart, twisting multiple strands together makes it much more difficult. This is why ropes are plied as well.

Why is there so much talk about thickness and strength? First, when you buy yarn for tufting, it must fit through the machine's needle. If you are using a cut-pile machine, the yarn also needs to be easily cut, or it will keep getting stuck in the machine. Tufters have found that there is a sweet spot in tufting two strands together of a medium-weight yarn (or three strands of a thinner yarn) that accomplishes a few goals.

First, two strands of a medium-weight yarn thread into the machine well. They don't get stuck, are easy to thread, and fill out a single tufted row nicely. Second, two strands won't break during tufting as easily as a single strand, especially if you are using a two-ply yarn. Third, using two medium strands instead of one thick strand makes the yarn surface more densely packed with less tufting.

Truthfully, you can tuft with almost anything that will fit through the needle. But it's a lot more fun to start out with success, build up your basic skills, and then experiment from there.

Below is a chart of the various names and weights of yarns with examples of how they might be labeled at your local yarn shop or online.

This chart describes yarn thickness and weight using the Craft Yarn Council (CYC) numbering system, the commonly known types, and the numbers of wraps per inch (WPI).

CYC	Type	WPI	Description	AKA
0	Lace	30–40	These are the lightest weight yarns, and are usually used for delicate projects such as doilies, shawls, and intricate lace patterns.	Thread, light fingering
1	Super Fine	14–30	These are slightly heavier than lace-weight yarns and are typically used for socks, baby clothes, and lightweight scarves.	Sock, fingering, baby
2	Fine	12–18	These are slightly heavier than super fine-weight yarns and are typically used for projects requiring a thin fabric, such as tops, shawls, gloves, and other light clothing items.	Sport, baby
3	Light	11–15	Slightly heavier than fine-weight yarns, these are typically used for light sweaters, hats, scarves, and other clothes.	DK, light worsted
4	Medium	9–12	Slightly heavier than lightweight yarns, these are typically used for afghans, cable-knit sweaters, and hats. They are seen as "all-purpose" yarns since you can use them for so many different types of projects.	Worsted, afghan, aran
5	Bulky	6–9	These are heavier than worsted-weight yarns and typically used for heavy winter sweaters, thick hats, and blankets.	Chunky, craft, rug
6	Super Bulky	5–6	These are some of the heaviest yarns and typically used for funky hats, scarves, and blankets. It's easy to learn how to knit with super bulky yarns since it's so easy to see the individual stitches. Once you get to this weight, you have to really experiment to see if it will work in a tufting machine.	Roving
7	Jumbo	1–4	The heaviest weight of yarns and typically used for accessories and home decor projects like blankets. This weight is also used for arm-knitting projects. It will almost never work in a tufting machine.	Roving

Note that roving is wool that has not been spun or twisted at all, so it pulls apart very quickly and probably won't work for tufting even if you have the right thickness.

YARN CONTENT
—

When selecting yarn to tuft with, it's essential to consider how the piece will be used. Is it intended as a wall hanging, as a floor rug in a high-traffic area, or as a coaster on a table? In addition to considering the aesthetic of your piece, you want to think about the wear it might be exposed to and what fiber content is the best match for that use.

Yarn is most commonly made of cotton, wool, or acrylic. In addition, you can find linen, bamboo, silk, cashmere, and dozens of fiber blends.

SYNTHETICS
—

Acrylic, polyester, and nylon are examples of synthetic fibers made from petroleum. Synthetic yarn is generally the least expensive. It can be soft and durable but is not biodegradable. Although most carpets are made of very durable synthetics, the majority of synthetic craft yarn is sold for making garments. While very soft, it is often not durable enough to hold up to being a rug. There are some good recycled synthetic yarns coming on the market that can provide durability and cost savings.

WOOL
—

The industry standard for rugs is wool, although it can get expensive. Wool is naturally very durable, flexible, and takes color very well. It is composed of long, crinkly fibers that make it bulky without being dense. It is fluffy and cushiony to walk on, and easy for your scissors to cut. Higher quality wool is typically made from longer fibers, which bond together more strongly and cut more cleanly. Longer fibers also keep wool from shedding too much.

left to right
1. 100% Wool, Fine weight
2. Reflect Yarn, Banana silk, Fine weight
3. Reflect Yarn, 100% New Zealand Wool, Medium weight
4. Sugar 'n Cream, 100% Cotton Yarn, Medium weight
5. Reflect Yarn, Eco-Cotton, Medium weight
6. Reflect Yarn, Recycled Wool and Viscose, Medium weight
7. Manos Del Uruguay, 100% Merino (Maxima), Super bulky weight
8. Wool and the Gang, Jersey Be Good, Bulky weight
9. Echoview Fiber Mill, Lanyard yarn, Medium weight
10. Manos Del Uruguay 100% Merino (Franko), Bulky weight

Cut-pile wool will stand up to years of use and won't look crushed despite regular wear. It is also a renewable resource that can be sustainably raised and harvested; look for wool producers who run humane and ecologically sound businesses. Interestingly, wool is also naturally flame retardant, making it great for hearth rugs. Wool rug yarn is generally too rough for making into clothing, while knitting yarn is prized and priced based on softness rather than durability. So steer clear of merinos and other specialty wools in your local knitting store and look for wool rug yarn sold by weight.

PLANT-BASED YARNS
—

A number of yarns are made from plants, including cotton, linen, bamboo, and banana. Cotton is relatively inexpensive, accessible, and incredibly durable. Cotton has been a staple of tough-wearing fabrics like denim and domestic necessities like rope, mopheads, towels, and more. The drawbacks to cotton for rugs are that it's not as dirt resistant as wool and its density makes it harder to cut, depending on the thickness. Cotton is also a renewable resource though its production requires a lot of water and other resources.

Linen is derived from the flax plant. It's stronger than cotton, and it produces a natural wax coating that adds a light sheen to finished projects. It can be very eye-catching when tufted, but it is much more expensive than cotton. While it can be used for tufting, it doesn't have any great advantages over less costly fibers like wool or cotton.

Banana silk is made from the waste of the banana industry, using the long fibers in the stalks and leaves of the plant. It produces a very silky and lustrous yarn that takes dye very well. Bamboo yarn has a similar feel and is also made from long fibers without the addition of synthetics. They both have the same density issue as cotton, so they work great with a loop machine but might require more finesse with a cut machine. If working with these denser yarns, it can be beneficial to sharpen your machine's scissors often.

Rayon, viscose, modal, and many other pseudosynthetic fibers have been made into clothing fabrics and knitting yarn. These use some plant materials and can feel soft like silk but are made using very chemically intensive processes that keep them from being environmentally friendly. We have not been able to test all of these yarns for durability and tuft-ability, so your mileage may vary.

RECYCLED AND SPECIALTY YARNS

—

There are several recycled yarns available to tufters. Numerous yarn companies are working with post-production or post-use fibers to create yarns that keep textiles out of landfills. From T-shirt cutoffs to sari silk, many makers take shredded fabric and twist it back into thread or yarn. A downside of these materials is that yarn spun from shorter fibers tends to be harder to cut and can dull your scissors faster. Still, once tufted, they create soft and durable rugs that have the extra advantage of benefiting the environment.

You can also make your own recycled yarn. Thrifted T-shirts and sweaters are a great source of material. Many knit sweaters can be unraveled, and the yarn used again in a tufting project. Homemade T-shirt yarn is soft and cozy when tufted into a pillow cover or collar.

CONES, HANKS, AND SKEINS

—

Rug yarn is often sold by weight and wound onto a cardboard cone. Coned yarn is excellent for tufting because the yarn pulls off the cone quickly without getting stuck. Also, cones contain a lot of yarn, so you can tuft large areas of color without having to rethread your machine. But yarn comes in other styles too, so let's have a quick lesson on the terminology.

A ball of yarn is what it sounds like, a round ball ready to use. It is usually wound up by hand and rolls around on the floor as you pull the yarn from it, rather than sitting neatly by your frame. A skein is an oblong ball, and a cake is more of a flattened ball. These are also ready to use and are a little more resistant to rolling away but are still somewhat difficult for tufting. But a hank is different. This is yarn that is sold in a long loop or a twist that will get hopelessly tangled unless you wind it into a ball or onto a cone before you try to use it.

If you are buying a lot of yarn that is not already coned, it can be helpful to buy a ball winder, which you can use to rewind your yarn onto an empty cone, dowel rod, or cardboard tube so that when you are tufting the yarn feeds smoothly into the machine. Fun fact: Empty toilet paper tubes fit on most ball winders, providing an inexpensive tube to wind onto.

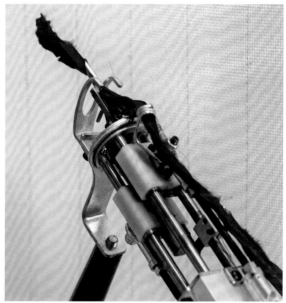

above left
This tufting sample shows the result of differences in the speed and density of tufting. The pink rows are all the same, but the teal stripes were tufted more slowly in the top half of the sample. Tufting slowly leads to many more strands of yarn in the same area, so those stripes appear thicker and denser.

above right
We used cut strips of a soft polyester-silk fabric to tuft a handbag. This fiber worked in a loop pile machine very smoothly.

EXPERIMENTATION

—

Experimenting with yarn can lead you to amazing and unique creations. There are no rules, but knowing some general guidelines can be helpful. Certain materials will tuft differently than others, some cut more easily, and variations in width can cause yarn to stick in the needle. Fibers and fabrics that are too thin will expose the backing cloth. You can prevent this by working with multiple cones and threading your machine with three or four strands simultaneously. Generally speaking, loop is always easier than cut since you are only testing one process at a time.

Turning up the speed dial on the tufting machine can help compensate for yarn that is too thin since fast tufting combined with a steady pace produces more tufts per inch. A higher speed also creates tension and tighter spacing between each tuft, making for a fuller pile.

above
We wound the strips around an umbrella swift (used by knitters to wind yarn) to make it easy to feed into the machine. Once it was threaded into the tufting gun, it was easy to tuft.

right
As you can see, the finished rectangle of fabric made a lovely clutch.

Essentially, any material can be used for tufting as long as it fits through the eye of the needle, so it's always helpful to run a test when using new yarn or yarn combinations to make sure it won't jam up or break while tufting. We've cut fabric strips, ribbons, raffia, and roving.

There are paper yarns, metallics, and even yarns that are actually tubes of extra fine–knitted yarn. The only line I don't cross are plastics, which might melt and jam up my machine. While I will knit with plastic bag yarn, I won't risk tufting with it.

Aliyah Salmon

Brooklyn, New York

Aliyah Salmon uses her extensive knowledge of complex color relationships and composition to illuminate objects of significance to the Black/Caribbean community. She highlights everyday objects associated with beauty by giving them the importance of a traditional portrait. These objects, such as a wide-tooth comb, are used prevalently in her work as symbols of Black femininity. Salmon also uses hand tufting and bead embroidery to incorporate slow crafts traditionally associated with the feminine.

Through her work, Salmon engages her viewers in nuanced conversations about the Afro Caribbean diaspora, Black women in America, childhood, isolation, and the subconscious.

left
Aliyah Salmon, *Grasp of Self*,
acrylic and wool on monk's cloth
hand tufted with punch needle

above
Aliyah Salmon, untitled
composition #7, detail. Acrylic
and wool on monk's cloth hand
tufted with Oxford punch needle

The Color Wheel

The twelve-step color wheel as we know it today is largely attributed to Johannes Itten, a Swiss-born artist, designer, and teacher who sought to simplify the explanation of color and color relationships for his elementary school students. He later took these teachings to the Bauhaus, a German art school active in the 1920s and 1930s and famous for developing the way fine arts and crafts are still taught in numerous art schools and universities today.

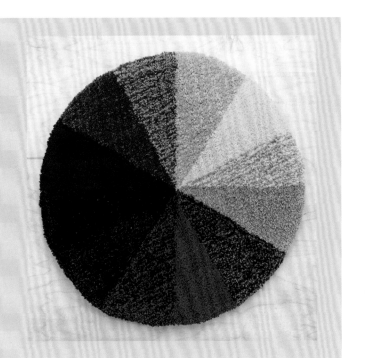

USING COLOR THEORY

The Color Wheel

Picking out colors for your design and seeing them come together on the rug can be one of the best parts of tufting. While many makers work intuitively and select colors based on various inspirations, other artists and designers use color theory to help create a finished piece's visual and emotional impact.

Using a guide like the color wheel can help you invent combinations that fit best with the intentions behind your design through an understanding of their relationship with one another.

The color wheel developed by Itten is a gradation from the primary colors of yellow, red, and blue. The colors change from yellow to red, red to blue, and blue to yellow, with three steps between each primary color. While there are other types of color wheels, the basic principles work for all of them.

There are three methods for using the color palette: analogous, complementary, and split complementary. Analogous colors are next to one another on the wheel. Combining three colors together can create a strong feeling of harmony and subtlety while also evoking

Pixels

—

Digital pixels are the most common form of an optical mixture. On every phone or computer screen, visual graphics are composed of small colored squares called pixels that allow the human eye to blend them into a single color when viewed from a distance.

These images show how pixels of different colors can create an optical mix. One shows the colors in boxes, as though you are zooming in very close and can see the individual pixels. In the other the colors appear more blended. This is part of the color scheme for the Bedside Rug project on page 108.

specific moods and seasons. The combination of yellow, yellow-orange, and orange can invoke a sunset, while blue-green, blue, and blue-violet can make for a moody interior.

Colors that are opposite each other on the color wheel are called complementary. Red and green, blue and orange, and purple and yellow are examples of complementary colors. Because of their extreme differences, they can make each other seem more vibrant when used together. Using a pop of yellow in a primarily purple composition can create a focal point or a surprise that draws viewers in.

Split complementary uses a focal color and rather than the one directly opposite on the color wheel, it uses the two colors on either side of it. Instead of blue and orange, you can use blue with red-orange and yellow-orange. Using split colors sparingly for details, or in paler shades than the main color, can keep this technique from being overwhelming or too busy.

Zapotec Rugs

—

Indigenous Zapotec people of modern-day Mexico have been weaving rugs on a loom for almost a thousand years. These patterns typically employ a limited palette of yarns that are mixed in different combinations to create the illusion of a much wider range of colors.

Illustration of the transparency effect

OPTICAL MIXING

—

Sometimes, you don't have every color of yarn you want to use, but you can create those colors using the technique of optical mixing.

The color wheel shown on page 64 was tufted using six colors of yarn. Only four sections are solid: yellow, blue, red-violet, and red. Since you can't mix colors with yarn the same way you would be able to with paint, optical mixing creates the illusion of a new color by using two different-colored yarns in the tufting gun at the same time. The solid yellow piece was made with two strands of yellow but the yellow-green was made with one strand of yellow and one of green. The closer the colors are to each other visually, the more blended they will look after tufting. Tufting black and white together won't make a smooth gray, instead producing a specked salt-and-pepper look.

This illustration shows an optical illusion called the transparency effect—the appearance that one color is overlapping the other. This technique of using a color that is a mixture of the other two is great for creating shadows, looking through windows, or creating an underwater effect.

One thing to note is that using cut or loop pile changes the look of the yarn's color. The way the light bounces off the strand of yarn is really different from how it hits a cut edge. Cut pile tends to look a little darker than the smoother loops. This can give you another way to play with shading within a composition.

A Cut Pile

Before the advent of the machine that revolutionized rug making, the creation of these beautiful floor coverings was a labor of love, performed entirely by hand. Rug hooking and knotting are two traditional techniques that have been passed down through generations of artisans, each with their own unique style and approach.

To make a rug by hand, the artisan starts by carefully selecting the highest quality yarns in their desired colors and textures. They then proceed to design the rug, using their knowledge and creativity to make a stunning work of art.

One of the key steps in the rug-making process is trimming, shaving, and planing the yarn ends. This requires a great deal of skill and patience, as the artisan must work carefully and precisely to ensure the yarn ends are evenly trimmed and that the pile of the rug is uniform.

The result of this meticulous attention to detail is an immaculate rug that is not only beautiful but also durable, with the quality of the yarn and the skill of the artisan ensuring that it will last for many years to come.

Sheep shears with a shearing guide produce a clean, level finished surface.

The critical thing is to keep experimenting and to keep track of what combinations really resonate for you. As you find colors in the world that strike a chord, take a quick photo for reference. These can be a starting point for a great rug or a series.

PILE HEIGHTS, SHAVING, AND SHEARING

"Pile" refers to the fibers of your carpeting, and it is used in reference to the carpet's density, height, and style. Higher pile means a more cushiony rug, while a short pile, especially in a loop style, can be the most durable. If a rug's pile is too short, you could see the backing fabric, and the rug would wear out more quickly. The range for most rugs is from ⅕ to ¾ inch (4 to 20 mm). This is similar to the height range of most tufting machines.

Tuft the World educator and artist Derek Hall is creating a clean edge between the two shades of blue by holding the clippers at a 45-degree angle and trimming the light blue edge (above), then repeating the process at the opposite angle on the dark blue edge (right).

Another way to play with pile height on cut pile rugs is by setting your machine to its greatest height and using clippers, scissors, or carving tools to make dimensional adjustments after you tuft.

Once a rug has been tufted, loops or threads can stick up above the surface, making it look irregular or untidy. Shaving your cut-pile rug creates a clean, level surface that lets your design shine through. All the strands are made an even height and fuzzy yarn ends are trimmed smooth.

This work can be done with scissors, but the cutting angle can be tricky. To cut evenly along the surface you can use bent handle or duckbill scissors. With a raised handle and wide bottom blade, duckbill scissors are designed to create a level cut and are great when cutting around tight corners.

Electric sheep shears, typically used for grooming sheep, can be used alone or attached to a shearing guide. Guides are beneficial when going over a large surface to ensure the height is consistent.

This family portrait by Veronica Cianfrano uses extensive carving work to create dimensionality among the elements.

If you are using shears alone, be extra careful about keeping them level; if you turn them into the fabric too deeply, they can create gouges that are really tough to repair. Shearing guides prevent unpredictable movements and give a more precise, flat trim.

CARVING

—

Carving techniques are used to define your cut-pile tufted rug dimensionally. The same tools used for shaving apply here—scissors, electric scissors, shears, or clippers. Some examples of carving are rounding outer edges, making space between different colors or design elements, or mitering abutting shapes. Carving into the rug surface can emphasize borders between colors, define text, or create various levels within an image.

There are different reasons for carving as you go—while you are still tufting your piece—and for working on a finished rug. When working on a tufted design with many different levels and shapes, it is easier to define each shape as the rug is being tufted because the surrounding area is still blank. This lets you work on designs without worrying about cutting into the neighboring color. This technique works well with advance planning, so you tuft the sections requiring the most rigorous carving first. The risk with this method is that since the rug has not been glued yet, you can pull the yarn out or cut into the cloth.

Carving rugs after they are glued is easier since the rug is no longer stretched onto the frame. You can bend and rotate it as needed during the carving process for more complex line work. You can also be less careful in terms of moving clippers or shears over the surface because you don't have to worry about accidentally pulling yarn from the fabric. On the other hand, it can be difficult to get an even surface once a piece is off the frame.

Electric clippers—like those used for hair or pets—can clean up a rug's edges or make crisp lines. As you tuft a straight line, strands can splay into adjoining areas. One fix is to carve along the edges of your shapes at opposing angles—as though you are cutting a V with the point at the center of the line. Start on one side of the line, cutting in at a 45-degree angle, so the deepest part of the clipper is at the middle of the line. Then rotate your rug and cut the same angle from the opposite side toward the line. Once they have met in the middle, there will be a solid visual border between the two sections.

Relief carving into a single-color rug creates dimension and can modify the value of the color in two ways, through the change in thread density and the shadows added to the more deeply cut areas. Low relief refers to shallow carving into a flat surface, for example, the V-shaped line emphasis discussed above.

High-relief carving not only uses a deep pile for more carving depth, it also refers to carvings that appear to be whole objects surfacing from the backing cloth itself. This is because there is little to no flat surface left, giving the overall design much more depth and more values from light to dark. With this technique, the color of the yarn can appear much lighter or darker, depending on how far it sticks out or recesses.

Venus Perez

Chula Vista, California

Venus Perez creates sculptural tufted portraits combining punch needle, machine tufting, and embroidery. Using the punch needle helps her achieve the wide variety of pile heights necessary to get the realistic dimension in her work.

A self-taught artist, Perez was drawn to fiber art through her maternal figures, who all sewed. She attributes her success to failure. When projects don't go according to plan, she sees it as a learning opportunity. The frustration that goes along with working through these problems is what causes Perez to start multiple projects at a time and conduct additional experiments that birth creative ideas.

The process of rug carving lends itself to this work ethic, as her tufted pieces often start out looking nothing like the intended outcome and get whittled down to their final forms over time. Perez refers to this as the beauty beneath the chaos.

The mixed technique works Perez produces are getting more adventurous as her disciplines grow. Her incredible skill and dedication to developing her craft are proving fruitful as she continues to enhance her sculptural works with more mediums and techniques.

top and middle
Venus Perez, *Frida Afterlife Glow* in progress, wool, porcelain, and copper wire made with punch needle and sculpting tools

bottom
Venus Perez, *Frida Afterlife Glow*, wool, porcelain, and copper wire made with punch needle and sculpting tools

How Punch Needle Became Tufting

—

In 1886, Ebenezer Ross from Toledo, Ohio, patented the first punch needle tool for creating looped pile fabrics. Punch needle embroidery quickly gained popularity as a way to create textured designs in a shorter amount of time compared to traditional hand embroidery.

The same year a wooden tool called Ye Susan Burr Hooked Rug Machine was created to mimic the stitches that were being created using a punch needle. Within a few decades, dozens of patents were filed for slightly different versions of rug-making tools. Several motorized punch needles were used by Catherine Evans Whitener's community for making bedspreads.

With all these inventions and adaptations around the globe, it's hard to say who first produced the motorized tufting machine. Tai Ping was a company in Hong Kong that created

an early handheld motorized tufting gun in 1956. Cabin Crafts in Georgia developed theirs in 1964. Hofmann, a German company, created their own around that time and they still produce one of the finest ones available.

In the last few decades, dozens of versions have been created, including the AK-I and AK-II, which were developed in the early 2000s. Due to the rise in popularity, new models have consistently been created and sold, with newer models having come to market probably since we wrote this. Proving that what feels like a brand-new invention is really a rediscovery of something that has been delighting crafters and entrepreneurs for centuries.

left
Ebenezer Ross,
Lion with Palms,
jute, wool, and
cotton hooked pile
rug, 1890–1900

opposite
Cléa Delogu,
Le Sac Plastique,
machine-tufted
acrylic yarn

GETTING STARTED AND FINISHING

o far, we've talked about the different types of tufting machines and how to use them, setting up your studio with a frame, choosing the right yarn, designing with color, and many of the additional tools that add to the rug-making fun. Now let's put it all together and walk through the process from beginning to end.

SETTING IT ALL UP
—

On your worktable, you should have your tufting machine, frame with clamps, yarn, tufting fabric, scissors, markers, a ruler, a threader or paper clip, and masking tape. Set up your frame and clamp it to the edge of your table.

STRETCHING THE FABRIC
—

The key to good tufting is having your cloth stretched as tightly as possible on the frame, like the head of a drum. When your cloth is supertight, your machine can glide freely across the fabric; it opens up the weave of the cloth so the needle can more easily find a place to tuft. Fabric that is not tight enough will tear easily or be difficult to work into.

Your fabric needs to be a few inches larger than your frame on all sides so you can grab onto it to pull it out from the center. Start by laying the fabric across the tacks at the top of the frame. It will catch easily onto the spikes and can hang there. Now firmly pull the fabric down and catch it on the lower spikes. Next, attach all four corners with a minimal amount of stretch. Connect the fabric to the tacks on the sides. Once you have the fabric attached, you will start tightening it bit by bit.

TIP - Clamping Your Frame
You will need the frame to be flush with the lip of the table so the fabric can be pulled past the bottom row of tacks. Use clamps to secure the frame to the table; if you are worried about the clamps digging into the table's surface, you can use a small cloth or towel as a pad between the clamp and the table.

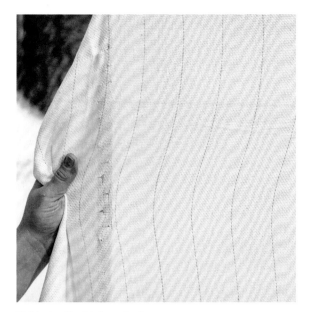
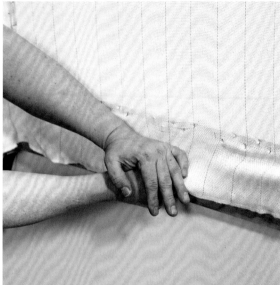

Tightening the fabric on the frame

TIP - Tufting Cloth Width
Tufting cloth is a special type of fabric that forms the foundation of your rugs. Usually made of polyester alone or blended with cotton, it is sold by the yard or meter but is generally much wider than other types of fabric. Clothing fabric comes in standard widths of 45 or 60 inches (110 or 150 cm), but tufting cloth is usually 157 inches (400 cm) since it is made for rugs that can be as large as a room. If you are using a tabletop frame, each yard of fabric is wide enough to make four rugs.

Tighten the left side by starting at the top left corner; lift the fabric slightly, pull it toward the outside of the frame, and restick it on the tacks. As you pull, the lines will warp somewhat to the left, as illustrated in the top left photo. Pull off the next section below the one you just pulled, and stretch it so that the lines straighten out as you move down the side. Repeat the same steps down from the top of the right side.

Next, you will stretch the fabric at the bottom. Grab the fabric with one hand and make a fist. Push down with your other hand as hard as you can, as illustrated in the top right photo. You should be applying as much force as you possibly can. Work from one side to the next, pulling straight down until the cloth is very tight. If there is still give in the cloth, you can pull the right and left sides a bit more, but constantly adjust the fabric down the side to keep the lines of your cloth straight. Your hand should glide smoothly across the cloth and it should feel tight.

One thing to note is that the corners will not be as tight as the rest, as it is the hardest area to stretch. Generally this isn't an issue because you can't tuft to the edge of the frame. It is best to keep a 2-inch (5 cm) border between the frame and the tufting area. This creates a boundary for tufting for two main reasons: As you work toward the edge, the tension of the fabric is inconsistent and

> **TIP - Take Care**
> Before you thread the machine, you MUST make sure the machine is off or unplugged. If the machine is on while you are handling it, you can easily trigger the tufting mechanism and get hurt.

can cause your machine to skip stitches or tear the cloth. And leaving a little space on the sides keeps you from hitting the frame with your machine's needle.

ADDING YARN

The yarn cones can be placed on your feeder or the floor. Thread each strand through an eye hook attached near the top of the frame; this will keep the threads from tangling and let the threads pull smoothly from the cone. It also means that the threads will be held away from the machine at an angle so that the yarn won't get caught in the machine's gears.

Finally, with the fabric stretched and the yarn hanging through the eye hooks, you will want to tape the edges of the frame so that the yarn doesn't get caught on the carpet tacks as you tuft. Masking tape works well for this. Don't use tape that leaves a residue, like duct tape.

USING THE MACHINE

Make sure the machine is at the right speed for you before you start tufting. If you are a beginner or have a complicated design with many curves or detailed areas, you'll want to turn the speed control knob on the bottom of the handle to the slowest setting. Then turn on the machine and press the trigger to test and make sure the speed is comfortable before threading the machine.

top left
Threading your machine, step one: Hold your machine so that the needle points away from you in your nondominant hand.

top right
Step two: Take the yarn that is hanging down from the side of the frame and push it through the large eyehole on the top of the machine.

bottom left
Step three: Take your threader (or a bent paper clip) and push the wire upward through the eye of the needle.

bottom right
Step four: Run the thread through the wire of the yarn threader and pull the yarn threader down through the eye of the needle, bringing the yarn with it.

THREADING YOUR MACHINE
—

Once you have set up your frame with the yarn feeders, you can line up the two strands of yarn together and leave them hanging down, ready to be threaded. (You can also sit in a chair and lay the machine on your lap.)

Hold your machine so that the needle points away from you in your nondominant hand (you will use your dominant hand to thread the machine). Be sure that the hand holding the machine is placed on the front handle (not the trigger) and that the weight of the machine is resting in the crook of your arm like a small dog. Be very careful not to place your fingers near the moving parts of the machine. Also, be aware of the power button, so you don't accidentally turn it on by pushing it into your arm or side (above, top left).

Take the yarn that is hanging down from the side of the frame and push it through the larger eyehole on the top of the machine (above, top right). Take your threader (or a bent paper clip) and push the wire upward through the eye of the needle (above, bottom left). Then run the thread through the wire of the yarn threader.

Finally, pull the yarn threader down through the eye of the needle, bringing the yarn with it (above, bottom right). Now your tufting machine is threaded! The yarn should extend an inch or two (two to five centimeters) past the hole of the needle. If there is too little, it might pull out and unthread; too much, and yarn will be wasted.

GETTING READY TO TUFT CHECKLIST
—

- Clamp the frame to the edge of the table.
- Stretch the fabric tightly over the frame.
- Tape the frame edges.
- Thread the yarn through the yarn feeder eye screws on the frame.
- Power off or unplug the machine.
- Thread the machine.
- Turn on the machine and check the speed.

START TUFTING
—

To begin tufting, it's important to remember that the needle and foot of the machine direct which way you can tuft. When the machine is upright, you can move it upward; if you want to tuft to the right, you have to rotate the tufting machine so that the needle and foot are in the correct position to move to the right. Turning the machine feels awkward at first but, once you have practiced a bit, you will get the hang of it. You should have a small area allocated on the side, top, or bottom of your stretched fabric where you can test out the machine and try a few different kinds of lines and different ways of holding the machine before going into your final design.

As you tuft, you have to maintain consistent pressure against the cloth. You should push so hard that the fabric bows out away from you, then pull the trigger and gently lift the machine as it tufts. If it feels like the machine is stuttering or kicking back or not moving smoothly, then you may not be pressing hard enough.

If you are tufting cut pile, you can pull the machine out of the fabric as soon as you are done tufting your first line, and then move the machine over to start tufting the next line of yarn. When tufting loop pile, you need to manually cut the yarn at the end of each row of tufting. As you reach the end of the row, pulling the machine away from the fabric too firmly will pull out the last few stitches you made.

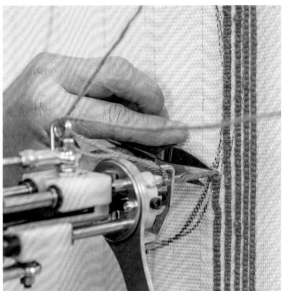

Instead, when you pull the machine out of the fabric, press a finger on the previous stitch (above left), and as you pull the machine away, the yarn will pull from the machine instead of the tufting. Then use your snips or small scissors to cut the yarn (above right). Many tufters wear their snips around their neck or let them hang from the frame to keep them handy during this process.

Keeping consistent pressure is the key to good tufting. Easing off the pressure will make the tufting look patchy, or the yarn will fall out of the cloth. If you are not pushing hard enough, it will feel like the machine bounces back at you. As you move the machine along the fabric, the feeling should be smooth; any sense of stuttering or bouncing means you should be pushing harder. In addition to these issues, a cut machine that is not pushed into the cloth enough can tear the cloth.

Be careful not to tuft too close to the edges of your frame. The carpet tack can scrape your knuckles. Putting tape over the carpet tack strips can minimize the risk of injury. If you make a mistake while tufting, you can simply pull the yarn out, realign the weave of the tufting cloth by rubbing your fingernail over the surface, making the holes smaller, and try again!

The most efficient way to tuft is in parallel rows. The space between rows of tufting can vary based on how many strands of yarn you are using or the thickness of the yarn. If you are tufting a lot of

above left
You can gauge your spacing by lining up the foot of the machine with the previous line of tufting.

above right
There is a gap that is a little too large between the last two lines of tufting, seen here from the back of the rug.

right
From the front of the rug, the gap between the rows is noticeable and needs to be filled in.

Type of Glue	End Use	VOC (Smell)	Application Method	Dry Time
Craft glue or PVA	Low traffic only	Little to no smell	Brush or roller	4 to 6 hours
Carpet/rug adhesive	High traffic	Some have a smell, some don't	Brush, roller, or trowel	6 to 12 hours
Latex (mask-making type)	Very flexible	High smell factor	Brush, roller, or trowel	6 to 12 hours

Characteristics of glues that can be used to finish tufted work

strands of yarn, you can space the rows a bit. I start by doing three test rows on the side of my fabric, with the rows about ¼ inch (6 mm) apart. After tufting the first row, line up the foot of the machine with the first row as shown in the top left photo on page 80.

The goal is to have the yarn fill out without any fabric showing through. If the fabric is visible, try closing the gap between the rows. On the other hand, tufting lines too closely together can warp the rug since the excess yarn will need room to spread out on the front and will distort the fabric. Forcing too much yarn can also tear the fabric. As you go, keep checking how the tufting looks on the front and, if you see an area that's too thin, add in some tufting in the gap (see images on page 80).

Because you have to cut the thread between every row when tufting loops, some folks like to tuft in one continuous motion to fill in an area using a tight S shape repeatedly. This is easiest going side to side since tufting in the downward direction means holding the machine upside down.

GLUING AND BACKING
—

Finishing always starts with gluing the back of the rug so the strands of yarn can't be pulled out. Choosing the right kind of glue starts with knowing what you want to do with your finished piece. Wall pieces or rugs that won't see a lot of foot traffic (like a small accent rug or throw pillow) can be glued with craft glue or PVA glue. For a piece in a high-traffic area, it's best to use glue specifically formulated for rug backing. For a garment, you will need a latex-based or flexible fabric glue. The first two options can be pretty stiff after drying, so if you are planning to wear something, you want a glue that will be flexible after it dries.

TIP - One thing to watch out for is some confusion around the term "carpet adhesive." At the hardware store there is something called carpet adhesive that is used to glue a finished carpet to the floor. The problem with this glue is that it can take weeks to months to dry and cure, it can be toxic, and it will crumble with handling over time. The glue you want is available online and will specify that it is for finishing tufted rugs. It will be strong enough to hold in all the strands of yarn and backing cloth where needed.

Every country has their brands and restrictions on adhesives. If a product listed above isn't available in your area or online, try testing other glues on sample pieces until you find one that meets your needs.

A note on adhesive toxicity: adhesives range in toxicity levels and odors; some can pose a respiratory threat. Please read the label on your chosen adhesive before use and follow the safety instructions. We recommend applying adhesive in a well-ventilated area and wearing a mask and gloves during application.

Having selected your glue, you can apply it with a brush, paint roller, or trowel. It is always best to glue the rug and let it dry on the frame since that prevents it from curling up. If you can't do that, tape the edges of the rug to a flat surface like the table or floor. Try to stretch it out when you are taping it. Then glue it and let it dry that way.

Apply a generous amount of glue to the back of your rug. Pay close attention to getting glue onto each tuft so it is secured to the cloth, since any missed spots might result in the tufts pulling out. Try not to spread glue outside of the tufted area—you want to push it right up to the edge of the tufting without going over since getting glue on the bare tufting cloth will make it stiff and difficult to turn or sew in finishing techniques. If the glue is too thick, you can remove the excess by scraping it off with a trowel, paint scraper, or scrap of cardboard. As the glue dries, it becomes quite hard, and any threads sticking out of the back or even just peaks of glue can create a lumpy surface, so smoothing it while it is still workable is important.

Once you have glued the rug, you have some backing options. You can let your piece dry as it is. This is not an issue if the back won't be seen, as in a wall piece, throw pillow, or appliqué patch. Or you can apply a plastic net or mesh backing. This is commonly seen on the backs of professional carpets one would find at a carpet or hardware store. Adding this to your piece during the gluing process will help flatten all the small yarn strands that stick up and give your piece an even surface. To add this backing, first apply glue to the entire surface of the piece, add the mesh backing while the glue is wet, then, using a brush or roller , smooth the mesh into the glued surface.

After doing a simple glue-up or adding a mesh backing, the next layer you can add is backing cloth. Backing cloths come in many different types of fabric, including nonwoven felts, woven cloth, nonskid fabric, and canvas. This is the part of your rug that lies on the floor. It is often made in colors that don't show dirt as much. Nonwoven fabrics (like felt) have the advantage that they won't unravel or fray at the edges. Final backing prevents the glue surface from scratching the floor and can add a nonskid feature to rugs on slippery surfaces.

You can apply cloth backing using the same glue you used on the back to hold in the yarn. After applying a thin layer to both the rug back and the backing cloth, let them get tacky, then lay the backing onto the rug. Start smoothing the cloth onto the rug back from the center out.

Another way to apply the final cloth is to use spray contact adhesive such as Roberts 8200. When shopping for spray glue, look for the phrase "contact adhesive" for the strongest bond. Follow the steps on the can, which typically instruct you to spray both pieces individually, wait for them to get tacky, then stick them together. This is a good method if you're in a hurry and need a quick bond. Again, lay the pieces out side by side, spray on the glue, and then turn the backing cloth over onto the rug back. Contact adhesive will usually let you reposition the fabric if your placement is initially off.

FINISHING
—

After cutting out and gluing your rug, the cut tufting cloth may be visible around the edges of your piece as well as the cut edge of your backing cloth. To create a clean edge, you can leave a small border of tufting cloth and after you are all done it can be folded over to the back side, glued down, and covered with cloth or binding (see top image on page 84).

Twill tape is made for this kind of work. It can cover both the raw edges of the tufting cloth and the backing fabric. This will not be visible from the front but adds a clean finish to your piece. Once finished, the edge of the rug will curl around, allowing the yarn to splay out into what's called a waterfall finish. Twill tape can be applied with the same glue you have used throughout the process or with a craft glue gun (see middle and bottom images on page 84).

above
Finishing the back by using twill tape to cover the raw edges

right
Applying twill tape using carpet adhesive

below
After applying the twill tape, use clamps to hold the tape in place while it dries.

If you're looking for an even more professional finish, you might consider sending your machine to a rug binder. Many cities have carpet repair businesses and most of these will be able to bind the edges of your rug by machine. They can add a serged or twill binding to your piece, and many offer a wide range of colors. This is an excellent option if you are selling your pieces and want the satisfaction of giving your client a professionally finished piece.

Finishing also includes shaving the rug surface, trimming loose threads, and/or carving around shapes to add definition. You can also create a cleaner design by weeding out stray colors—separating individual pieces of yarn that have strayed into an adjacent color field, making for a fuzzy border (see image at bottom left). This lack of definition is a natural part of tufting but leads to a less sharp design. Each strand that is out of place is coaxed back toward its proper area; while time-consuming, it can make a huge difference in the aesthetics of the final piece. For this process, we recommend using a large needle, comb, crochet hook, or closed scissors.

All of these finishing techniques add to the look and the long-term durability of

top
Left to right: twill tape, serged/whipstitch, waterfall

bottom
Weeding the different colors using a comb

the rug. Most folks find a finishing method that works for them and stick to it.

SAFETY PRECAUTIONS WHILE TUFTING
—

Like many other arts, tufting has side effects that can impact your health. Often something that doesn't bother you the first few times you experience it can lead to issues when you do it all the time. Most tufting machines make as much noise as a power drill or loud sewing machine. The noise is insufficient to require a safety warning, but we recommend earplugs or noise-protection headphones. When using an industrial tufting machine, ear protection is required to protect your hearing.

Another health concern is fiber inhalation, which we mentioned earlier. Yarn is made of loose fibers rolled together to create a continuous strand. When each strand moves through the head of the tufting machine, it sheds a tiny amount of fibers into the air. To avoid breathing these in, you can use a combination of airflow and an air purifier. Working between a fan and a purifier will direct the fibers out of your space and take them out of the air. A simpler solution is wearing a dust mask while you tuft.

Tufting machines can be quite heavy. If your wrists, feet, or back begin to ache, take a break and stretch! We recommend wearing motocross fingerless gloves and comfy nonskid shoes, and maintaining good posture while tufting.

MAINTENANCE

—

The essential element of machine maintenance is regularly oiling your tufting machine, regardless of the model. Your tufting machine will have specific recommendations for how often to add oil and where but it must be used regularly to ensure it stays in good working order. We recommend that you oil your machine every time you use it. As a general rule, apply oil to every part of your low-pile machine that moves. Apply a few drops of oil to the metal bars in front of and behind the white square bearings and the rotating bearings at the ends of the upper and lower bars.

High-pile machines need to be oiled more frequently than low-pile machines because they run at higher speeds. We recommend oiling your high-pile machine every few hours during use. As a general rule, apply oil to every part of a high-pile machine that moves. Focus on the metal bars in front behind the white square bearings and the blade near the needle.

Whether a low- or high-pile machine, once it is oiled, turn the machine on to evenly distribute the oil, adding more drops as needed until the machine runs smoothly. You can't over oil, so don't be shy.

Tufting machines can use 3-in-1 oil, sewing machine oil, or mineral oil.

TROUBLESHOOTING

—

These are some common issues folks have when tufting, and possible solutions.

ISSUE: YARN FALLS OR PULLS OUT OF THE NEEDLE.
SOLUTION: The yarn likely isn't being fed into the machine smoothly enough. Make sure you use coned yarn or yarn that can pull off a ball without getting snagged. Check where the yarn might be getting caught between the cone and the machine.

ISSUE: THE YARN ISN'T GOING INTO THE CLOTH OR SEEMS TO FALL OUT WHILE TUFTING.
SOLUTIONS:
- Push harder. The foot of the machine should stay in strong contact with the cloth.
- Always move your tufting gun in the correct direction, turning the machine when making a curved line of tufting (see page 120).
- Your yarn likely isn't being fed into the machine smoothly enough. Make sure you use coned yarn that can pull off a ball without getting snagged. Check where the yarn might be getting snagged between the cone and the machine.
- The tufting cloth isn't stretched tight enough on your frame.
- The foot to needle hole relationship is off. This can happen if the machine has been dropped or after incorrectly adjusting the pile height. When the needle is in its most forward position, the hole should just be in front of the foot. If the hole is too far forward, it will shred the cloth; if it is too far behind, the yarn will not stick in the cloth.

ISSUE: CUT PILE MACHINE ISN'T CUTTING THE YARN.
SOLUTIONS:
- The yarn you are using isn't a good fit. Soft yarns can be difficult for the machine to handle. Sometimes you can combine one strand of a softer yarn with one that is easier to cut.
- Adjustments need to be made to the mechanism that controls the scissors. The front piece should be loosened and moved toward the back of the machine. This will cause the scissors to close more. On the other hand, if the scissors are not opening all the way when

they retract back, you may need to move the scissor opener forward. Adjustments should be made in small increments until you find the sweet spot.

ISSUE: CLOTH RIPS DURING TUFTING.
SOLUTIONS:
- You may be using the wrong cloth. It's best to use fabric made specifically for machine tufting. Monk's cloth and burlap don't have sufficient durability and will rip easily.
- You are not moving the machine in the correct direction. Make sure to turn the machine when changing direction (see page 120).

ISSUE: LOOPS AREN'T A CONSISTENT LENGTH.
SOLUTIONS:
- The cloth you are using may not be a good fit for tufting. If it is not strong enough or has a loose weave, then there won't be consistent tension holding the loops in place.
- You are tufting in the same spot on the fabric for too long, so the machine is pushing more than one loop into a single hole. As you tuft you always have to be moving steadily so each tuft of yarn can go into its own space in the weave.
- The pressure of the machine against the cloth isn't consistent.
- The tufting cloth isn't stretched tight enough on your frame.

ISSUE: THE MACHINE MAKES A "BEEPING" SOUND.
SOLUTIONS:
- The yarn you're trying to tuft is too thick or not a good fit.
- Something is causing the machine to jam. This usually means the yarn is caught somewhere or a part is bent, preventing the parts from moving smoothly.

opposite
Aliyah Salmon, *Grasp of Self*, acrylic and wool on monk's cloth hand tufted with punch needle (detail)

Industrial Carpet Making and Broadloom

It is not really possible to pinpoint the first machine-produced carpet. Different companies were constantly trying to improve the weaving and tufting processes to make more affordable rugs and carpets. The year 1791 saw the opening of the first woven carpet mill in Philadelphia by William Sprague. Other carpet mills opened throughout the American Northeast, including the Beattie Manufacturing Company in Little Falls, New Jersey, which operated under various names until 1979. Erastus Bigelow in 1839 invented a power loom for weaving carpets that tripled carpet production in just a few years.

New types of power looms and design mechanisms were springing up almost every year. That same era saw the rise of the mechanical sewing machine, which revolutionized the mass production of textiles. These developments met up with the chenille tufting craze in Dalton, Georgia, in the early twentieth century (see page 48).

Due to the demand for more bedspreads, Glenn Looper of Dalton developed the first mechanized tufting machine. Looper modified the single-needle Singer sewing machine to tuft the thick yarn into unbleached muslin without tearing the fabric, and attached a knife to cut the loop. Other makers quickly realized that they could add more needles to each machine, first adding four, then eight, twenty-four, and more needles to make the parallel rows of tufted cloth.

Later, with the end of World War II, workers were returning to work, rationing of textiles was over, and the sudden demand for beautiful home goods made the perfect market for tufted rugs and carpets. American textile technicians took their knowledge of the technology of tufting, weaving, and early carpet making and merged these with yardage machines that could feed fabric rolls into the tufting process. The result was a new generation of machines that tufted with dozens of needles that could punch into fabric as it simultaneously flowed through the machine.

Needing a constant supply of more yarn pushed the development of synthetic yarns and in 1958 DuPont released nylon, a petroleum-based yarn that could be dyed to any color and was incredibly durable and stain-resistant. Tufting went from a $133 million per year business in 1951 to $1 billion dollars in 1963.

Today, tufted products make up more than 90 percent of the total carpets and rugs produced in the world. Less than 2 percent of rugs are woven, and 6.7 percent comprise all other methods, such as knitted, braided, hooked, or needle punched. And Dalton, Georgia, continues to be the center of the carpet industry; it is still known as the "Carpet Capital of the World."

left
The John & James Dobson Carpet Mill. Begun in the 1850s, this was one of the largest carpet companies in the nation and the chief employer in Philadelphia's heavily industrialized Falls of Schuylkill region.

below
Tufted nylon carpet produced by DuPont in the 1950s

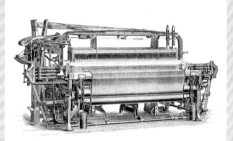

above
This open shed fancy loom from 1891, made by Knowles Loom Works in Warren, Massachusetts, is an early example of the constant invention and development in textile production.

Practicing the Techniques

2.1

As you work through the projects, you will build your skills so you can grow into making things more complex. The first projects emphasize the basics, with each one adding a new technique or tool. Your first project will be a simple floor mat made on a tabletop frame measuring 30 × 30 inches (76.2 × 76.2 cm).

Denja Harris

San Diego, California

Denja Harris draws on personal experience and artistic intuition to create work that explores identity, vulnerability, and the intersection of race and gender. Working in Southern California, she uses a bold, graphic style that is an outgrowth of her experience of otherness and the disconnection faced as a Black woman.

Harris's tufted pieces are vibrant and playful yet convey complexity through their intricate designs and layered textures. Challenging traditional notions of design, she strongly emphasizes the role of negative space, elevating it as a critical component of her creative process. Her care for the environment has led to her use of dead stock materials— remnants of industrial production that are often discarded—as a way to keep these yarns out of the landfill.

With beautiful textures and imaginative designs, Harris's work invites viewers to embrace vulnerability and nurture their softer side. Her unique vision asks us to reconsider the rules of art and design and to challenge our perceptions.

top
Denja Harris, untitled machine-tufted upholstered chair

bottom
Denja Harris, *Negative Space 2*, acrylic, polyfill, and yarn waste, machine tufted using a cut-pile tufting machine

FLOOR MAT

Small floor mats are a lovely way to create a welcoming entry point to a home, a respite to warm your feet on a cold floor when getting out of bed, or a soft place to stand at a bathroom sink. They also provide opportunities to create design moments in your space, a focal point with color and texture. This design will be made with cut pile–either use a cut-pile machine or, if using a Duo machine, make sure the scissors are engaged.

FINISHED SIZE: 24 × 24 inches (61 × 61 cm)

FOR THE TUFTED DESIGN:

Tufting frame (approximately 30 × 30 inches/76.2 × 76.2 cm) with clamps

Tufting cloth (36 × 36 inches/ 91.4 × 91.4 cm)

Straightedge or ruler

Sharpie markers

Masking tape

Threader

3 to 4 pounds (1.3 to 1.8 kg) yarn (two cones each of four separate colors)

Cut-pile or Duo tufting machine

Scissors or thread snips

FOR FINISHING:

Rug glue

Spreader or small paint roller

Binder clamps or spring clamps

Nonskid backing cloth

Face mask

Masking tape

Roberts 8200 contact adhesive

For the tufted design:

Set up your frame and stretch the fabric (see page 64). As you tuft, the fabric will become looser on the frame; you can always stop tufting and restretch the cloth to get a good work surface.

—

Outline the rug using a straightedge and marker, leaving space between the edge of your work and the frame. A good rule is to leave a 2-inch (5 cm) fabric gutter inside the frame untufted. This helps your tufting be consistent and reserves a fabric edge for finishing the rug. [**FIG.1**]

—

Draw a simple design without too much detail or tight curves on the fabric and note where you want specific colors. Don't forget that the final rug will be reversed, so if you use any symbols, letters, or numbers, they must be drawn backward. Use the masking tape to cover the area of carpet tack near the yarn feeder to prevent yarn snags, as shown on page 76.

—

Select the two strands of yarn you'll be starting with—they can be the same color or a mix of two yarns. Thread them through the feed loops on the frame, and then into your machine. [**FIG.2**]

—

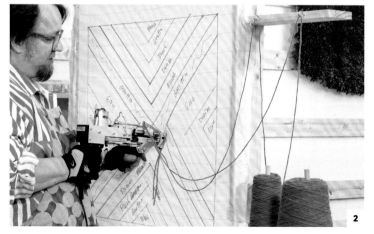

3

It can be helpful to tuft a test line in the gutter. Start tufting by pushing the machine's needle into the cloth near the bottom edge of the frame and raise the machine in a straight line up the fabric. Make sure you are pressing hard enough—if you are having trouble getting a consistent line of stitches, you might need to push harder. This is also an excellent time to adjust the speed dial on the machine.

—

After a couple of test lines, start making your design. Press the needle into the fabric at the bottom of the area you want to fill and steadily lift it up along the fabric while maintaining pressure on the fabric all the time. [**FIG. 3**]

—

It's good to overshoot the top of the area you are filling in a bit. You can pull out the excess strands that are outside your design.

—

Once you complete a line, go back to the bottom and create another line next to the first about ⅛ inch (3 mm) apart. Try to make each line parallel to the previous one.

—

Depending on the shapes you are filling in, some sections may have lots of short lines, and others will have nice long parallel rows. Go ahead and fill in all the areas that use the color you have started with. When you are ready to change colors, pull the current thread out of the machine, replace the new color cones on the yarn feeder, thread them through the eye hooks, and then thread them into the machine.

—

4

The back of the rug when fully
tufted and trimmed

Check your work periodically on the other side. You are looking for areas that appear a little thin, where you can fill in between a couple of rows that you tufted a little too far apart. Areas you haven't tufted might appear smaller since the yarn from adjoining sections will crowd over into the empty area. Don't worry; once you've filled those areas, you'll have a clear division between the sections.

—

Continue in this way until all the areas of your design are filled. [**FIG. 4**] Cut any extra-long pieces from the back of your rug, but wait until after gluing to work on the front so you don't accidentally pull out too many strands.

—

Congratulations!! You made a rug! Run your hands over it and feel proud of yourself. [**FIG. 5**]

—

For finishing:

Once you finish tufting, you'll need to complete the rug by putting glue on the back to hold all the pieces of yarn in place.

—

Leave the piece stretched tightly on the frame and apply the glue evenly across the threads with a spreader or roller, getting some glue onto every strand. Be careful not to get glue onto the tufting fabric outside the design since this fabric will be needed to finish the rug. [**FIG. 6**]

—

A nice finish for this rug will include nonskid backing. Once the glue on the back of the rug is dry, cut the rug out of the cloth, leaving a small border of 1 inch (2.5 cm). Fold over the excess tufting cloth to the back side and glue it in place with rug glue. To secure these edges while the glue dries. you can use clamps to hold the tufting cloth in place. This is called a waterfall finish.

—

5   The finished rug

6

Cut a piece of nonskid backing cloth slightly larger than your finished rug. Set up a space to work outside and wear a face mask to avoid breathing in any mist. Mask off the edges so the glue doesn't get on the yarn sticking out. Spray contact adhesive onto the backs of the rug and the nonskid cloth. Let them become a little tacky, then lay the backing cloth onto the rug. Once they are put together,

they will be difficult to reposition, so make sure the rug and backing match up.

—

Smooth the backing out from the center and let it dry flat. Drying time depends on the glue and the humidity, but it should not take longer than a day. Trim away the excess to leave a clean edge.

Felicia Murray

Portland, Oregon

Felicia Murray's work springs from a fascination with nature, growth, and decay throughout the natural world. She is a transplant from the American Northeast to the Pacific Northwest, both locales known for their lush landscapes and varied ecosystems. She currently works in Portland, Oregon, examining the relationship between personal growth and natural evolution, reflecting on the constant changes in the organisms around us. Murray employs a wide range of media and techniques, including tufting, to bring her visions to life.

Her landscape-inspired installations are created through the artful combination of felting, tufting, and sewing, inviting the viewer to engage with the work through the same tactile curiosity of children exploring tidepools and undergrowth. The sprawling clusters of yarn and fabric seem to take on a life of their own, appearing both flourishing and deteriorating.

An advocate for the environment, Murray's work serves as a powerful reminder of the interconnectedness of our inner lives and outer habitats, highlighting the importance and impermanence of the natural world.

left
Detail of *Art Is Home*

overleaf
Felicia Murray, *Art Is Home*, wool cut-pile and punch needle tufting with felted components

Floor Rugs

2.2

In this section, we will look at making functional
rugs for various uses in the home. Each rug will
incorporate a new style or technique appropriate for
the space it will inhabit—bedroom, kitchen, or entryway.
Smaller rugs are incredible for bathrooms,
the bedside, and as accents throughout your home.
You can also make rugs for specific areas that
have a unique layout.

opposite: Selby Hurst Inglefield, *Care for You*, wool on hessian created with a punch needle

BEDSIDE RUG

Having a small rug by the bed keeps your feet cozy in winter and can add a touch of color to brighten your mornings. Since tufting uses multiple strands of yarn at a time, you can create a heathered or dappled effect by using different colors held together. This project will use this technique to create a gradient effect.

FINISHED SIZE: 18 × 24 inches (45.7 × 61 cm)
To make a rug that is larger than your frame, follow the instructions on page 115.

FOR THE TUFTED DESIGN:
Tufting frame (approximately
   30 × 30 inches/76.2 × 76.2 cm)
   with clamps
Tufting cloth (36 × 36 inches/
   91.4 × 91.4 cm)
Straightedge or ruler
Sharpie markers
Masking tape
Threader
3 to 4 pounds (1.3 to 1.8 kg)
   yarn (ten cones of yarn,
   one color each)
Cut-pile or Duo tufting machine
Scissors or thread snips

FOR FINISHING:
Rug glue
Spreader or small paint roller
Spring clamps or binder clips
Small paintbrush
Nonskid backing cloth
Face mask
Masking tape
Roberts 8200 contact adhesive

For the tufted design:

Set up your frame and stretch the fabric (see page 64).

—

Outline your rug with the straightedge and marker, drawing your design and marking off your color choices. This is not necessary but it helps if you have to stop tufting mid-project and come back to it a few days later. This gradient rug will need to have one section fewer than the number of colors you are using. Ours uses ten colors, so the design is broken into nine sections. [**FIG.1**]

—

Use the masking tape to cover the area of carpet tack near the yarn feeder to prevent yarn snags, as shown on page 76.

—

Thread the machine with colors one and two held together and start tufting from the bottom right corner, moving the machine upward in long, steady rows. [**FIG.2**]

—

When you get to section two, rethread the machine with colors two and three.

—

Continue in this way across the rug—the next section will be made with colors three and four.

—

As you work your way across, practice getting the lines of tufting parallel to each other. You can use the foot of your machine to line up each row.

—

To make sure the top and bottom edges are even on the final rug, you can overshoot a little on each line of tufting. Once you are finished, you can pull out any threads that are outside the desired shape.

—

Trim any strands on the front that are overly long and clean up the extra threads on the back.

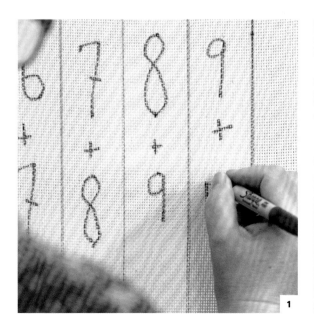

For finishing:

After you finish tufting your rug, glue the back while it is still stretched on the frame.

—

Apply the glue evenly across the threads with a spreader or roller, getting some glue onto every strand. Be careful not to get glue on the fabric outside the design since once the glue has dried it is very difficult to cut or bend, and we will use this fabric edge to finish the rug.

—

After the rug is dry, cut it out from the tufting fabric, leaving 1 inch (2.5 cm) of unglued fabric around the border of the design.

—

TIP - Letting your rug dry on the frame keeps it from curling up as it dries. If you took your piece off the frame before gluing, you could always restretch it when you are ready to glue.

Create a waterfall edge on the rug by folding the unglued tufting fabric toward the back of the rug and gluing it down with rug glue. Use a small paintbrush to apply the glue to the edge. Let it get tacky and then fold it over and press into place.

—

Use clamps to hold the glue until it dries. [**FIGS. 3-4**]

—

This is a great rug to finish with a nonskid backing material if it is going to be used on a slippery floor. We used a felt backing with nonskid dots every few inches.

—

Cut a piece of backing cloth slightly larger than your finished rug. [**FIG. 5**]

—

Set up a space to work outside and wear a face mask to avoid breathing in any mist.

—

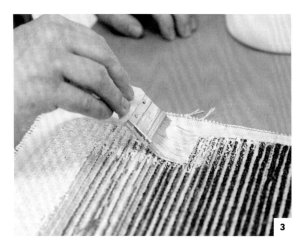

3

4

Mask off the edges so the glue doesn't get on the yarn sticking out. Spray contact adhesive onto the backs of the rug and the backing cloth.

—

Let them become a little tacky, then lay the backing cloth onto the rug. Once they are put together, they will be difficult to reposition, so make sure the rug and backing match up.

—

Smooth the backing out from the center and let the glue dry. Trim away the excess to leave a clean edge. Turn over and admire your work. [**FIG. 6**]

below
Cléa Delogu, *Le Ramen*, machine-tufted acrylic

5

6

KITCHEN MAT

This kitchen mat will be tufted using loop pile. Loop pile can make for very defined edges and increased durability. We'll also show you how to create curved designs using straight lines. This rug will be finished with a waterfall edge and nonskid felt backing cloth.

    Working with a loop stitch involves one extra step that cut stitches do not–snipping the yarn at the end of each row. Since loops are all one continuous piece of yarn, it's up to you to cut the yarn off before going on to the next row.

– – – –

FINISHED SIZE: 18 × 24 inches (45.7 × 61 cm)
To make a rug that is larger than your frame, follow the instructions on page 115.

FOR THE TUFTED DESIGN:

Tufting frame (approximately
    30 × 30 inches/76.2 × 76.2 cm)
    with clamps
Tufting cloth (36 × 36 inches/
    91.4 × 91.4 cm)
Straightedge or ruler
Sharpie markers
Masking tape
Threader
Loop-pile or Duo tufting machine
3 to 4 pounds (1.3 to 1.8 kg) yarn
    (two cones each of three colors
Scissors or thread snips

FOR FINISHING:

Rug glue
Spreader or small paint roller
Face mask
Roberts 8200 contact adhesive
Nonskid backing cloth

For the tufted design:

Set up your frame and stretch the fabric (see page 64).

—

Outline your rug with the straightedge and marker, drawing your design and marking off your color choices. This is not necessary but it helps if you have to stop tufting mid-project and come back to it a few days later. If you want to use an image as a guide, as seen in Fig. 1, make sure to reverse the image before you print it, so it will match the layout on the back of the cloth. [**FIG.1**]

—

Use the masking tape to cover the area of carpet tack near the yarn feeder to prevent yarn snags, as shown on page 76.

—

Thread your yarn through the eyeholes on the frame so they hang down next to the tufting area.

—

Take the yarn that is hanging down from the side of the frame and push it through the larger eyehole on the top of the machine. Take your threader (or a bent paper clip) and push the wire through

the length of the needle from the tip toward the back of the machine. Catch the yarn coming through the eyehole with the threader and pull it through the needle until it hangs out the front of the needle.

—

Make a few practice rows in the gutter if this is your first time tufting loops. Start by pushing the needle into the fabric, then tufting in a continuous line up the row.

—

When you get to the stopping point, pull the machine out gently from the cloth, so only a little yarn pulls out. Then grab your snips and cut the yarn. You can cut the yarn ¼ inch (6 mm) from the fabric or leave a long tail if you like, and then trim the back before adding glue.

—

TIP - Keep your small scissors or snips handy by wearing them on a ribbon around your neck.

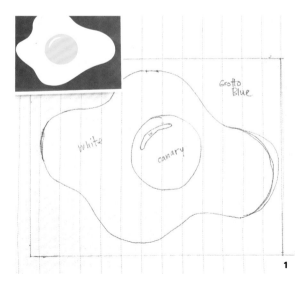

1

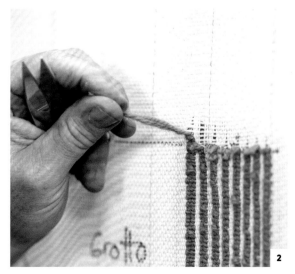

2

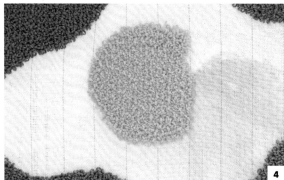

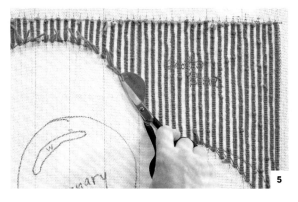

It is easier to pull out a couple of loops than to go back and add one or two stitches at the end of the row, so it makes sense to go over the edge of your design until you have a good feel for where to stop. Still, be careful pulling out stitches since a hard pull could remove more than you meant to. [**FIG. 2**]

—

Continue tufting in straight vertical lines from bottom to top, stopping when you get to a border in the design.

—

As you fill in a curved shape like the egg yolk, you'll be tempted to turn the machine to draw curved lines. Instead, keep filling the shape with vertical lines from bottom to top. [**FIG. 3**]

—

Once you have filled everything in on the back side, it will look like a rounded shape on the front. [**FIG. 4**]

—

When you finish tufting, take a moment to check the front for any stray loops that are outside the lines or any extra-long loops that need to be cut back. Then trim any long threads on the back side in preparation for gluing up. [**FIG. 5**]

For finishing:
The kitchen is another place where a nonskid backing can be helpful. After the piece is glued and the edges are finished, apply the backing cloth with spray adhesive. Follow the gluing, waterfall edge, and backing instructions for the bedside rug (see page 110). [**FIG. 6**]

TIP - Steps for Making a Rug Larger Than Your Frame

If you want to make a rug that is larger than your frame, one option is to tuft your rug in sections. You can stretch a large piece of cloth on your frame, draw a portion of your design, tuft it, and then move the fabric to draw and tuft the next section.

Stretch your fabric as normal, with the excess fabric hanging down from the bottom of the frame. Tuft the top portion of your design, staggering the bottom ends of your rows so that there will not be a hard line where the new tufting joins up after moving the fabric on the frame. [FIG.1]

Once ready to move on to the next section of tufting, take the unfinished rug off the frame. Move your tufted cloth up and lay the finished work over the top of the frame so it hangs down on the other side of the frame. The tufted part of the rug will hang over the top toward the back so that the unfinished area will be centered in the frame. Stretch the sides and bottom of the working fabric onto the carpet tack, making sure the fabric is as straight as possible.

Use a board and clamps at the top of the frame to secure the tufted portion of the rug. Place the board across the top edge of the frame on top of the finished tufting and use the clamps to secure it in place. [FIG.2] >>

1

2

Once the fabric has been moved and stretched, you can continue drawing your design. In this example, we used a projector and traced our design onto the fabric, lining it up with the existing tufting when we moved it. [**FIG. 3**]

Since the finished rug is larger than the frame, you can glue it in sections the way you tufted it. Alternatively, you can lay the rug face down on a worktable and tape it to the table, stretching it as much as you can while you tape it down, then glue it. As long as you don't untape it until it is dry it shouldn't curl.

3

Trish Andersen

Savannah, Georgia

Trish Andersen's vibrant, larger-than-life tufted works are bursting with texture and color. Born and raised in Dalton, Georgia—the "Carpet Capital of the World"—it is only fitting that she would become an early adopter of tufting in the United States, developing a sophisticated process and visual language all her own.

Andersen's work is often characterized by echoing shapes evocative of the layered strata seen in geological formations but with a chaotic color scheme of an artist's used paint palette. She brings that oppositional duality to much of her work— playful and eerie, sleek and wild, gentle and jarring. Working digitally with tools like Procreate, Illustrator, and Photoshop, she drafts her designs prior to tufting them and keeps a running stash of ideas for future projects.

The scale of her work combined with her love of texture and color helps make it so immersive. Andersen's stair runners are particularly noteworthy, being both practical and feeling like an art installation with the way they treat the shape of the stairs as part of the design.

Andersen hopes to one day create tufted furniture and is thankful to have the opportunity to continue tufting, as she loves it to her core.

top
Trish Andersen, *Rainbow Runner*, tufted using mixed yarns

bottom
Trish Andersen, *Steady Stream*, hand tufted and sewn using mixed yarns

CURVES AND WAVES

While most rugs are rectangles, part of the fun of making your own is being able to design irregular shapes that enhance the area they inhabit. This project uses cut and loop piles to create visual interest and contrast, but you can make it in all loop or all cut if you prefer. It will also explore the risks and benefits of driving your tufter around the design to make curved outlines and filling them in.

When tufting cut pile, the direction of the tufting path does not make a difference to the finished look since all of the strands blend together, but loop pile shows a little more of the process.

How you move the tufting machine affects how the loops sit on the front of the rug. It doesn't matter which technique you use for tufting round shapes, but if you use a loop machine, you want to be consistent and use the same method throughout.

This project can be designed to use a variety of colors, which can be helpful when you have a bunch of colors left over from other projects. We used ten colors in this design, but you could make it with as few as three.

_ _ _ _

FINISHED SIZE: 24 × 24 inches (61 × 61 cm)
To make a rug that is larger than your frame, follow the instructions on page 115.

FOR THE TUFTED DESIGN:
Tufting frame (approximately
    30 × 30 inches/76.2 × 76.2 cm)
    with clamps
Tufting cloth (36 × 36 inches/
    91.4 × 91.4 cm)
Straightedge or ruler
Sharpie markers
Masking tape
Threader
3 to 4 pounds (1.3 to 1.8 kg)
    yarn in various colors
Cut-pile and loop-pile or Duo
    tufting machine
Scissors or thread snips

FOR FINISHING:
Rug glue
Spreader or small paint roller
Mesh backing (32 × 32 inches/
    81.2 × 81.2 cm)
Hot glue gun
Spring clamps or binder clips
Felt backing cloth
Face mask
Roberts 8200 contact adhesive

Tim is tufting from right to left, so the machine is positioned on its left side, with the bottom of the machine facing the camera.

1

For the tufted design:

Set up your frame and stretch your fabric (see page 64).

—

Draw your outline and design using the straight-edge and markers, leaving a 2-inch (5 cm) gap between the edges of the design and the frame.

—

Use the masking tape to cover the area of carpet tack near the yarn feeder to prevent yarn snags, as shown on page 76.

—

Take the yarn that is hanging down from the side of the frame and push it through the larger eyehole on the top of the machine. Take your threader (or a bent paper clip) and push the wire through the length of the needle, from the tip toward the back of the machine. Catch the yarn coming through the eyehole with the threader and pull it through the needle until it hangs out of the front of the needle.

—

Since we will be tufting in different directions, take a moment to practice a horizontal line in the gutter above or below your design. The key to tufting in a particular direction is turning the whole machine in the direction you are moving. If you are tufting a horizontal line from right to left, you have to turn the machine on its side. [**FIG.1**] To tuft from left to right, you need to flip the machine onto the other side. Make a few rows of stitches from one side to the other.

—

Once this feels comfortable, try making a curve. Start with the machine upright and push into the fabric near the bottom of the fabric. Tuft a row moving up the side of the fabric, and then turn the machine onto its side as you continue tufting until you make a horizontal line across the top.

—

Outline the first shape by driving the machine around it. You can make this line in short sections as you gain confidence with making curves. It's usually uncomfortable to tuft with the machine upside down (and it can cause your yarn to become tangled in the machine). It's better to approach all shapes from side to side or bottom to top until you are comfortable moving the tufting gun in all directions. [**FIG. 2**]

—

Once your curved shape is outlined, you can fill it in by repeating those curves or filling it with straight rows of tufting.

—

For contrasting shapes, you can change from a cut-pile to a loop-pile machine. Fill each shape using the same motions from beginning to end. Outline the shape using loops and then fill it in by following that original curve. Again, you can tuft longer or shorter sections of the curves based on what's comfortable, stopping a line and starting it from another approach as needed.

—

Each row of tufting will follow alongside the previous one, repeating the same path, until the shape is filled in.

—

Continue tufting the various curves and sections until the design is complete.

—

Trim away excess strands to prep for gluing. [**FIG. 3**]

—

top
Since Tim is tufting at a downward angle, he has positioned the machine so it is almost upside down.

2

3

For finishing:

Glue the back while it is still stretched on the frame.

—

Apply the glue evenly across the threads with a spreader or roller, getting some glue onto every strand and making sure not to spread it over the edge of the tufting.

—

The mesh backing should be cut to the size of your frame so you can attach the backing to the carpet tacks. This will keep the mesh backing pushed against the tufted piece until the glue dries. Use a brush or roller to smooth the mesh into the wet glue.

—

Once the glue is dry, you can cut the design out of the fabric, leaving at least a 1-inch (2.5 cm) border all around. Additionally, cut the mesh backing flush with the design to eliminate bulk when folded over the tufting fabric.

—

To get the edges to lie flat, you will need to cut into the border from the outer edge toward the design every couple of inches so the entire border becomes a series of flaps that can be glued down one at a time. [**FIG. 4**]

—

Fold over the edges and hot glue the flaps down. Hot glue usually dries quickly enough that you won't need to clamp it, but you can use a weight (like a book) on top of the flaps to help them lie flat. [**FIG. 5**]

—

Glue the rug and backing cloth together and trim the edges following the directions on page 110. [**FIG. 6**]

4

Wall Hangings

2.3

These projects are made to hang on the wall as decoration or works of art. They don't have to have the same durability as something that's going to get walked on, and they allow for more experimentation and playfulness. This section will explore mixing rug design with other decor elements, and each project will include a suitable hanging process.

opposite: Melissa Monroe, *Face Hider*, wool and vintage fabric hand tufted and sewn (detail)

Andie Solar

Seattle, Washington

Slovakia native Andie Solar started working with punch needle (a manual tufting technique) in 2017. Her work embraces a midcentury minimalism that features clean lines and an exacting carving technique. She recognized a need for punch needle kits that feature sophisticated designs that are also fun to make. Her business, Myra and Jean, has been focused on introducing punch needle through online and in-person classes and she has also written the book *Pretty Punch Needle* to share the craft with even more folks.

Solar's artwork brings a contemporary and eclectic attitude to the traditional art of hand tufting. This combination of past and present allows her art and her kits to inspire and connect with viewers.

Her monochrome palette and the repetitive movement in her tufted and punch needlework have a calming effect, encouraging one to slow down and focus on the present moment. The meditative quality of Solar's work is further emphasized by its focus on honoring the home, the space of comfort and relaxation.

top
Andie Solar, *Circles*, machine-tufted and hand-sculpted acrylic with beading on a wooden dowel

bottom
Andie Solar, *Sunburst*, machine-tufted and hand-sculpted acrylic on a wooden dowel

PICTURE FRAME OR MIRROR

A tufted picture or mirror frame is a beautiful and eye-catching way to decorate a room. This project can be done with various levels of woodwork skills. You can buy a premade mirror or frame with a large wooden border and attach your tufted edge directly to it with glue and staples. You can also make a custom frame using several methods. Once your mirror is picked out, you can create a wood backing for the mirror using thin plywood, lauan, or MDF. A sturdy backing will provide structure and protection to the mirror and is an easy surface to attach the hanging hardware to. Another source of backing is thin wood, chipboard, or stiff cardboard, which can sometimes be found in thrift stores or recycled from broken furnishings or frames.

We wanted to make a sturdy piece, so we chose plywood backing. We secured the mirror to the wood with construction adhesive, and the tufted frame is glued and tacked to the wood backing around the mirror. The shape of the finished piece can be created by cutting out the wood with a jigsaw, band saw, or even a handsaw. Alternatively, you can start this project by tufting a frame shape and then, after it is complete, trace the rug onto the backing material to cut out.

If you prefer to start with an existing frame, you can start at the beginning and skip the section on making the backing.

- - - -

FINISHED SIZE: 24 × 30 inches (61 × 76.2 cm)

FOR THE TUFTED DESIGN:

Sheet of paper (24 × 30 inches/ 61 × 76 cm); this can be cut from newspaper or made by taping smaller sheets together

Straightedge or ruler

Sharpie markers

Scissors

Mirror

Tufting frame (approximately 30 × 30 inches/76.2 × 76.2 cm) with clamps

Tufting cloth (36 × 36 inches/ 91.4 × 91.4 cm)

Threader

Masking tape

3 to 4 pounds (1.3 to 1.8 kg) yarn in three colors

Tufting machine of your choice

FOR THE TUFTED BACKING:

Rug glue

Spreader or small paint roller

Mesh backing (32 × 32 inches/ 81.2 × 81.2 cm)

Hot glue gun and glue sticks

Clamps

FOR THE MIRROR BACKING:

Piece of ¼-inch (6 mm) plywood (24 × 24 inches/61 × 61 cm)

Marker

Jigsaw, band saw, or handsaw

Clamps

Eye protection

Face mask

Work gloves (optional)

Sandpaper (220 or P-180 grit)

Construction adhesive

Spreader

FOR PUTTING IT TOGETHER:

Rug glue, hot glue or construction adhesive, or upholstery stapler

Level

Pencil

French cleat

Wall anchors (if needed)

Screwdriver or drill

Spring clamps

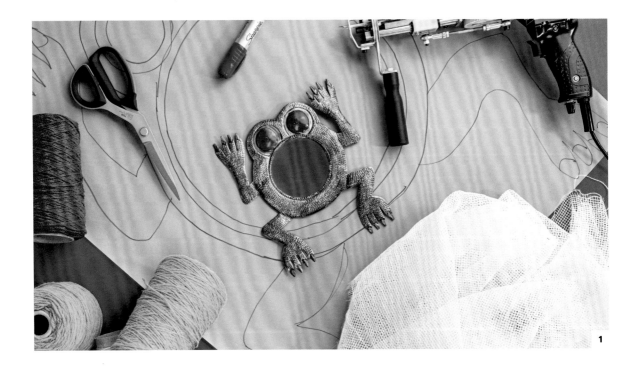

1

For the tufted design:
Create a drawing of your mirror frame on the sheet of paper and cut it out. Trace the space where the mirror will go within the drawing. You will use this cutout as a template to trace onto your tufting cloth and again later onto the wood backing. [**FIG.1**]

—

Set up your frame and stretch your fabric (see page 64).

—

Trace the outline of your paper template onto the tufting cloth. If you are using an existing frame, you can trace that shape directly onto the fabric. Leave a 2-inch (5 cm) gap between the edges of the design and the frame. Trace the outline of the mirror in the location it will be placed since you won't want to tuft into that area. Use the masking tape to cover the area of carpet tack near the yarn feeder to prevent yarn snags, as shown on page 76.

—

Thread your machine, following the directions on page 77.

—

Start by tufting the details like the fingernails, the eyes, and the outline of the mirror. Tufting smaller areas first lets you control their placement and size. You can tuft these areas either by using straight lines or by filling in with curves.

—

Outline the eyes with an accent color by tracing around them from the base of the circle to the top on each side. Remember to maintain your pressure as you outline the circle. If some angles are difficult, try tufting in shorter arcs. Tuft at least two rows around each eye in order for the outline to stand out.

—

As you tuft your main color, keep an eye on making the edges of your design neat and defined.

—

Continue tufting until the design is complete, leaving the space for the mirror untufted. Trim away excess strands to prep for gluing.

For the tufted backing:
Glue the back while it is still stretched on the frame. Apply the glue evenly across the threads with a spreader or roller, getting some glue onto every strand and making sure not to spread it over the edge of the tufting. Take care not to get the glue onto the fabric where the mirror will go.

—

Place the mesh backing against the back of the piece and use a spreader or roller to smooth the mesh into the wet glue.

—

Once the glue is dry, cut the design out of the fabric, leaving at least a 1-inch (2.5 cm) border of tufting fabric all around. Trim the mesh backing up to the edge of the glue to reduce bulk in the finishing. Where your design curves, cut the border from the outer edge toward the design every couple of inches to create a series of flaps that can be glued down one at a time with hot glue.

—

TIP - If your tufting cloth is visible from the front after the glue has dried, you can carefully paint the fabric edges to match the color of your yarn so it won't distract from your piece.

If you have sharp points or corners, cut the fabric to each point, so the flaps can lie flat more easily.

—

Follow the same cutting pattern around the edge where your mirror will go. [**FIG.2**]

—

Glue all the flaps and edges down, pulling them to the back so that none of the tufting cloth will be visible from the front. Use clamps to hold the flaps in place while the glue dries.

Note: If you are using an existing frame, stop here and continue to page 132, "For putting it together."

2

3

For the mirror backing:

Lay your tufted work or paper template on the plywood and trace it. Then trace the inner shape where the mirror will go. [**FIG. 3**]

—

If using a handsaw or jigsaw for cutting the wood backing, clamp the wood to a sturdy table with one side hanging over the edge by several inches.

—

Put on your eye protection, face mask, and gloves. Breathing in wood dust can be harmful, and today is not a good day to get a splinter in your eye! Work gloves are optional but really nice when you don't want to get splinters in your fingers.

—

Use your saw to cut out your frame. When cutting into a deep shape, it can be helpful to cut it into sections. [**FIG. 4**]

—

After cutting one side, unclamp and rotate the frame piece to the next side, continuing until you have all four sides finished.

—

Although this piece of wood will be completely covered by the tufting, it's a good idea to sand off the outer edges to remove the roughest particles. [**FIG. 5**]

—

Apply construction adhesive to the back of the mirror and spread it out. You can use a small piece of scrap cardboard for a spreader if you don't have one. Press the mirror onto the backing and lay some books or weights on top to keep the mirror in contact with the wood.

4

5

TIP - If you're using this as a picture frame, use photo-safe double-sided tape or spray adhesive to attach the photo to a stiff backing (like mat board), then attach the backed photo to the wood with spray adhesive.

For putting it together:

You can attach your finished tufting to the backing board or frame using hot glue, rug glue, construction adhesive, or staples. [**FIG. 6**]

—

If your backing board or frame is thick enough, staple your piece through the front in between the tufts with an upholstery stapler.

—

If you are using glue, wait until the tufting and the mirror have dried, then spread the adhesive over the wood backing. Add some adhesive to the back of the tufting as well.

—

Let the adhesive get tacky and press the pieces together. Add some weights, so the rug stays in contact with the backing plywood.

—

After everything is dried and cured (check your adhesive instructions for complete cure time), turn the mirror face down so you can lay out and attach the hanging hardware.

—

This mirror will be hung using a French cleat. A French cleat is a way to secure an artwork or other object to a wall; often made of wood, it is simply a board that gets cut in half lengthwise at 45 degrees. One half gets attached to the wall and the other to the mirror, or whatever object you're hanging. The two halves of the cleat thus get fitted back together to hold the object in place.

—

Mark where you want to attach the upward-facing cleat to the wall using the level to make sure your piece will hang correctly. Screw the cleat to the wall with a screwdriver or drill.

—

Attach the downward-facing portion of the cleat to the back of the piece. Run a bead of construction adhesive along the cleat and use spring clamps to hold it to the piece until the glue cures. [**FIG. 7**] Be sure to place the cleat far enough down on the back of the tufted piece so that the wall cleat will not be visible when the piece is hung.

—

Once the adhesive on the cleat is cured, you simply set the downward-facing cleat onto the upward-facing one and your piece is up!

right
Rebecca Coll, *Yellow Snake Mirror*, hand-tufted yarn on wood and mirror

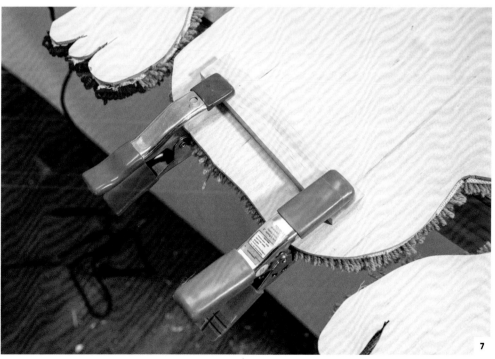

AJ Peterson

Los Angeles, CA

AJ Peterson's art blends their queer identity with spirituality, nostalgia, and fantasy. Peterson was drawn to tufting due to its tactile and physical nature, which requires intense focus while also engaging the senses. This balance of physical and mental focus enables Peterson to delve into their inner world and create pieces that reflect their confidence and happiness.

Peterson's background in design infuses their work with a graphic quality, making amazing use of fonts, framing, and pop iconography to express adult identity while retaining a childlike wonder.

The clean, crisp tufted and carved text in Peterson's work showcases their meticulous skill as a craftsperson and gives us an exciting glimpse into this rich inner world.

above
AJ Peterson, *Lover Boy 1*, machine-tufted and carved wool

right
AJ Peterson, *Queer of Hearts*, machine-tufted and carved wool

ART WITH TEXT

Creating lettering that is easy to read takes a little practice. A cut-pile machine can produce really clean results since the outline of the letters can be carved after you're done tufting. If you are not ready to start carving, a loop machine makes neat lines, because the yarn won't blend at the borders.

One of the funny things about making something from the back is that while you are working on it, you see the image backward. A common issue folks have is planning words or letters in their design and forgetting that they will be reversed on the finished product.

This piece will use a plywood backing to support an organic shape, like the previous project.

– – – –

FINISHED SIZE: 26 × 26 inches (66 × 66 cm)

FOR THE TUFTED DESIGN:

Sheet of paper (24 × 30 inches/ 61 × 76 cm); this can be cut from newspaper or made by taping smaller sheets together

Straightedge or ruler

Sharpie markers

Scissors

Tufting frame (approximately 30 × 30 inches/76.2 × 76.2 cm) with clamps

Tufting cloth (36 × 36 inches/ 91.4 × 91.4 cm)

Masking tape

Threader

3 to 4 pounds (1.3 to 1.8 kg) yarn in six colors

Tufting machine of choice

FOR THE TUFTED BACKING:

Rug glue

Spreader or small paint roller

Mesh backing (32 × 32 inches/ 81.2 × 81.2 cm)

Small paintbrush

Spring clamps or binder clips

FOR THE WOODEN BACKING BOARD:

Piece of ¼-inch (6 mm) plywood (24 × 24 inches/61 × 61 cm)

Marker

Jigsaw, band saw, or handsaw

Clamps

Eye protection

Face mask

Work gloves (optional)

Sandpaper (220 or P-180 grit)

FOR FINISHING:

Hot glue or construction adhesive or upholstery stapler

Scissors or comb

Duckbill or bent handle scissors or electric clippers

Handheld vacuum

FOR HANGING:

Level

Pencil

French cleat

Wall anchors (if needed)

Screwdriver or drill

Spring clamps

TIP - Tufted lettering needs to be more than one line thick to stand out and be legible. Block lettering is the easiest initially, but you can start using scripts or other more complex fonts as your skills increase. Make sure the lettering is in reverse when tufting so it will read correctly on the front.

For the tufted design:

Draw your design on the sheet of paper and cut it out to form a template. Use a dark marker to draw your design to make it easier to trace through the tufting cloth.

—

Set up your frame and stretch your fabric (see page 64). Leave a 2-inch (5 cm) gap between the edges of the design and the frame.

—

Trace the outline of your paper template onto the tufting cloth. Tape the paper to the front of the frame and trace the marker lines on the back of the cloth. If your design is complex, you can color in sections so they are easy to distinguish from one another as you are tufting. [**FIG.1**]

—

Use the masking tape to cover the area of carpet tack near the yarn feeder to prevent yarn snags, as shown on page 76.

—

Thread your machine, following the directions on page 77.

—

Start by tufting the words so you can make adjustments without feeling boxed in. It's okay if the letters seem a little too spread out since once you tuft in the space around them they will tighten up.

—

When outlining the letters or other shapes, use a consistent number of rows to keep the thickness of the line consistent. Work from the center of the design outward when creating outlines and drop shadows.

—

Once you have completed the main design, fill in the background using vertical lines. Tracing around shapes with the machine can be hard on your arms and shoulders—save that for times when it matters, like outlining something.

—

Continue tufting until the design is complete.

—

Trim any strands on the front that are overly long and clean up the extra threads on the back.

For the tufted backing:
Glue the back while it is still stretched on the frame. Apply the glue evenly across the threads with a spreader or roller, getting some glue onto every strand and making sure not to spread it over the edge of the tufting.

—

Place the mesh backing against the back of the piece and use a spreader or roller to smooth the mesh into the wet glue.

—

Once the glue is dry, cut the design out of the fabric, leaving at least a 1-inch (2.5 cm) border all around. Cut the mesh backing to the edge of the glue to reduce bulk in the finished edge.

—

Create a waterfall edge on the rug by folding the unglued tufting fabric toward the back of the rug and gluing it down with rug glue. Use a small paintbrush to apply the glue to the edge, let it get tacky, and then fold it over and press into place.

—

Use clamps to hold glue until it dries.

For the wooden backing board:
Lay your tufted work or paper template on the plywood and trace it. If using a handsaw or jigsaw for cutting the wood backing, clamp the wood to a sturdy table with one side hanging over the edge by several inches.

—

Put on your eye protection, face mask, and gloves. Breathing in wood dust can be harmful, and today is not a good day to get a splinter in your eye! Work gloves are optional but really nice when you don't want to get splinters in your fingers.

—

2

3

Use your saw to cut out the backing board. When cutting into a deep shape, it can be helpful to cut it into sections.

—

After cutting one side, unclamp and rotate the frame piece to the next side, continuing until you have all four sides finished.

—

Although this piece of wood will be completely covered by the tufting, it's a good idea to sand off the outer edges to remove the roughest particles.

For finishing:
Using hot glue or construction adhesive, attach your finished tufting to the backing board. You can also staple your piece through the front in between the tufts with an upholstery stapler if your backing board is thick enough for the staples.

—

Use scissors or a comb to separate tufted areas using a technique called "weeding." This will really help define the two different areas. [**FIG. 2**]

—

Using scissors or electric clippers, trim a small bevel on the outer edge of each letter to create clean lines. [**FIG. 3**] When using electric clippers or other electric shears, wear a mask since they create a lot of airborne fibers. Vacuum as you go to remove fiber dust.

—

Finish your rug by trimming any stray threads on the surface. [**FIG. 4**]

For hanging:
Follow the directions on page 132 for attaching a French cleat.

4

SCULPTURAL CARVING

This project will focus on using carving tools to create three-dimensional effects. Carving can strengthen borders between color elements, clean up edges, or make a three-dimensional landscape on the rug's surface. Since this is a smaller piece, it will be backed with fabric and have a small amount of wood attached for hanging. For this project, you'll be carving as you tuft. Some people find this to be a more straightforward method rather than waiting until all the tufting is finished.

– – – –

FINISHED SIZE: 26 × 26 inches (66 × 66 cm)

FOR THE TUFTED DESIGN:
Tufting frame (approximately
    30 × 30 inches/76.2 × 76.2 cm)
    with clamps
Tufting cloth (36 × 36 inches/
    91.4 × 91.4 cm)
Straightedge or ruler
Sharpie markers
Masking tape
Threader
3 to 4 pounds (1.3 to 1.8 kg)
    yarn in five colors
Cut-pile, Duo, or AK-III tufting
    machine
Sheep shears and shearing
    guide (optional)
Scissors (embroidery, bent
    handle, and duckbill)
Small tufted piece for practicing
    (optional)
Electric clippers
Handheld vacuum
Face mask

FOR FINISHING:
Rug glue
Spreader or small paint roller
Backing cloth (optional)
Hot glue gun and glue sticks

FOR HANGING:
Pine board (1 × 4 × 18 inches/
    2.5 × 10.2 × 45.7 cm)
Upholstery stapler
Eye screws or D hooks
Framing wire
Hammer
Gallery hooks

For the tufted design:

Set up your frame and stretch your fabric (see page 64). Leave a 2-inch (5 cm) gap between the edges of the design and the frame.

—

Trace the outline of your design onto the tufting cloth. Plan your design by pile height. Draw out your design and designate yarn colors for each area as usual. Then, mark areas from lowest to highest pile. [**FIG.1**] Use the masking tape to cover the area of carpet tack near the yarn feeder to prevent yarn snags, as shown on page 76.

—

Thread your machine, following the directions on page 77.

—

Set your machine to the highest pile and make some test tufts in the margin. Try out the various pile settings to ensure you get the desired lengths for your design.

—

If you are using an industrial machine like the AK-III, you will be able to achieve a much higher pile throughout and you can use the sheep shears and the shearing guide to level out large areas after tufting.

—

Start by tufting the lowest pile height area of your design.

—

Use the bent handle scissors to trim a bevel around the edge of the tufted area. [**FIG.2**] If you have a test piece of tufted fabric, you can practice this and the next step on it first.

—

Use the electric trimmer to even out the surface of the tufted area. [**FIG.3**] Be careful not to make a hole in the tufting cloth as you trim.

—

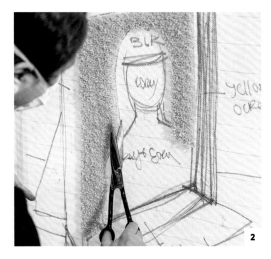

Since you can't draw your design onto the yarn, you can "sketch out" your design by using embroidery scissors to trim a small amount along the surface where you will want to cut away a large amount later. Cut into the piece slowly, making shallow cuts as you work, vacuuming as you go. [**FIG. 4**]

—

Wearing a face mask, use the clippers to carve down each section. It can be helpful to use the clipper guard attachments to ensure the same level is carved throughout for smaller flat areas.

—

For rounded areas, start carving at the shortest part first, holding the clippers at an angle and moving it upward toward the highest part of the curve. It's important not to carve at too steep of an angle at this stage. Make sure you hold the clippers as close to parallel with the surface as possible and rely on scissors to clean up the edges.

—

If your design has more than two pile heights, tuft the next-shortest section, ending with the highest pile height. After each section of tufting, stop and trim the edges and clean up the surface with the clippers.

—

Continue the process of tufting, carving, and vacuuming until the desired effect appears. Be careful not to trim areas too short, otherwise, the tufting cloth can show through. [**FIGS.5-7**]

For finishing:
Vacuum the surface again, then glue and finish the back of the piece as you like with a backing cloth following the directions on page 110 or leave the glue raw if you prefer.

—

Once the glue is dry, you can cut the piece out, leaving at least a 2-inch (5 cm) border of extra fabric. Use the clippers to make crisp edges and clean up any small areas, being careful not to go too deep and reveal the tufting cloth.

—

Finish the edge of the rug after carving is complete by folding it back and hot gluing the overhang on the edges in a waterfall edge, as before.

—

Be careful using the carving tools to create a level surface after gluing the edges. The irregular surface of the glue and the slight bulk of the extra cloth on the back of the piece make it difficult to get a consistent pile height.

—

5

6

For hanging:

Position the pine board across the upper back of the piece and affix the piece by stapling it to the board through the front of the design. It helps to part the pile and pull it away from where you plan to staple it and then fluff the pile over it.

—

Attach the eye screws to the board at both ends and run the framing wire through the hooks, twisting the ends of the wire together when you have the right length.

—

Hammer the gallery hook into the wall and hang your piece.

EXTENDING YOUR ART WITH MACRAMÉ

Macramé is a way of making coarse lace, hanging art, or decorative fringe by knotting cords in geometrical patterns. It integrates beautifully with wall rugs as a way to hang them, create fringe edges, or add ornamentation.

In this project, we will tuft a wall hanging with a design that continues into macramé hanging below. An easy way to integrate macramé and tufting is to connect the macramé threads into tufted loops. In our design we wanted to continue the zigzags down from the tufting into the macramé. Since the tufting yarn is a little thin for macramé, we decided to use it doubled to make thicker knots.

This design uses two macramé knots–the lark's head and the double half hitch. The lark's head is used to connect the macramé strands to the tufting. All of the remaining work is done in double half hitch knots worked back and forth in sections.

－－－－

FINISHED SIZE: 10 × 24 inches (25.4 × 61 cm)

FOR THE TUFTED DESIGN:

Tufting frame (approximately
   30 × 30 inches/76.2 × 76.2 cm)
   with clamps
Tufting cloth (36 × 36 inches/
   91.4 × 91.4 cm)
Masking tape
Sheet of paper (24 × 30 inches/
   61 × 76 cm); this can be cut from
   newspaper or made by taping
   smaller sheets together
Sharpie markers
Straightedge or ruler
Threader
3 to 4 pounds (1.3 to 1.8 kg)
   yarn in five colors
Loop-pile or Duo tufting machine
Scissors or thread snips

FOR FINISHING:

Rug glue
Spreader or small paint roller
Mesh backing (32 × 32 inches/
   81.2 × 81.2 cm)
Hot glue gun and glue sticks

FOR THE MACRAMÉ:

40 pieces of yarn 4 yards
   (3.6 m) long; ten for
   each section
Crochet hook US E/4 (3.5 mm)
Small rubber bands
Sewing pins
Wide-tooth comb

For the tufted design:

Set up your frame and stretch your fabric (see page 64). Leave a 2-inch (5 cm) gap between the edges of the design and the frame. Use the masking tape to cover the area of carpet tack near the yarn feeder to prevent yarn snags, as shown on page 76.

—

Using paper, Sharpie marker, and a straightedge, draw the design for your project and tape it onto the back of the tufting cloth, so it shows through the fabric. Trace the design onto the cloth and label the yarn colors, so it's easy to keep track of when tufting.

—

Thread your machine, following the directions on page 77.

—

Our design is entirely loop pile, but if you would like to make yours cut, you can, as long as you make the bottom two rows loop pile so there will

be a place to attach the macramé. You can use both kinds of stitches for the rest of the design or keep it all loop if you prefer. When tufting loops, you will need to cut the yarn close to the fabric at the end of each line of tufting.

—

Start tufting on one side and fill in each stripe of color. As you get comfortable tufting you may find you prefer to work from left to right or vice versa, based on which hand is dominant.

—

Since this is a loop project you can either follow the zigzag lines or fill in the shape using vertical lines, but it is a good idea to pick one method and use it throughout the project for continuity.

—

Continue tufting until you are finished.

—

Trim and clean up the extra threads on the back.

3

For finishing:

Finish the piece as you like with backing cloth or leave the glue raw if you prefer. We are using mesh backing to create a clean finish on the back of the piece.

—

Glue the back while it is still stretched on the frame. Apply the rug glue evenly across the threads with a spreader or roller, getting some glue onto every strand and making sure not to spread it over the edge of the tufting.

—

Place the mesh backing against the back of the piece and use a spreader or roller to smooth the mesh into the wet glue.

—

Take extra care to ensure all the loops at the edge are firmly glued down without going over the edge.

—

Once the glue is dry, you can start adding the macramé. You can't do this before it is glued or you will pull the loops out.

For the macramé:

Attach the first color of yarn strands to the bottom row of loops using a line of lark's head knots.

—

Fold each macramé strand in half. Insert a crochet hook through one of the loops on the edge of your design. [**FIG.1**] Loop the strand of yarn at the center point onto the crochet hook [**FIG.2**] and pull 1 to 2 inches (2.5 to 5 cm) of the strand through the tufted loop.

—

Set the crochet hook aside and pass the remainder of the strand through the large loop you created. Pull the strand so the knot tightens around the loop. That's a lark's head! [**FIG.3**]

—

Continue adding all the strands of the first color. You can add all the strands at once or add them in sections, but you need to have at least the first section in place to start the macramé work.

—

Once the strands have been added, you can wind each piece around a couple of fingers and put a rubber band around each bundle so they don't get tangled. Leave about 18 inches (45 cm) of length to work with.

—

The section on the far right will continue along the zigzag design from left to right. Since you folded each section of yarn in half to make the lark's head, each working piece now contains two strands.

—

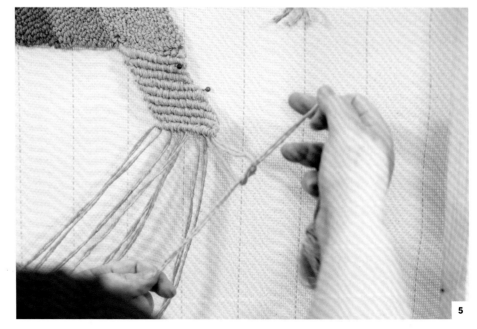

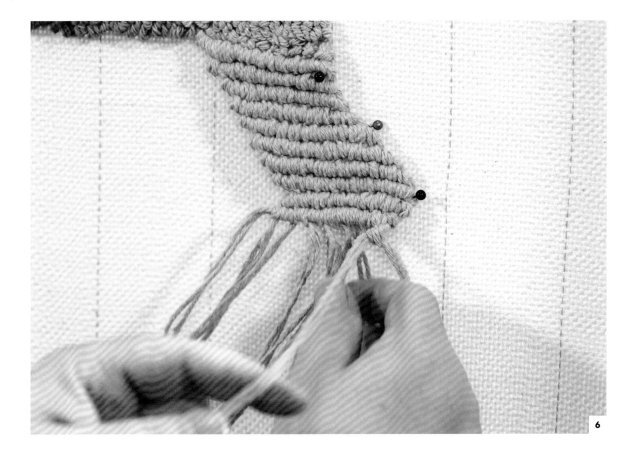

6

Next you are going to work a row of double half hitch knots from left to right.

—

Start at the left side of the section again and continue making rows of double half hitch knots going to the right for the next eight rows. As you work, the weight of your knots might start to pull the design out of shape. You can use pins to keep the design in place.

—

Now it's time to start working in the opposite direction in order to make the zigzag. From the ninth row to the sixteenth, work the double half hitches from right to left.

—

Continue making rows until the macramé measures about 8 inches (20 cm). [**FIGS. 4-6**]

—

Repeat the same pattern for the next three sections, starting each one going in the opposite direction from the one next to it. After finishing all four sections, cut the ends, leaving a fringe of 2 to 3 inches (5 to 8 cm), and brush it out with a wide-tooth comb for a soft finish.

Silk Stocking Rugs of the Labrador Coast

In the early 1900s, English doctor Wilfred Grenfell and American artist Jessie Luther used new ideas about occupational therapy to create a cottage rug industry in isolated fishing communities on the far northeastern coast of North America. Grenfell had decided to dedicate his life to improving living conditions in areas reliant on deep-sea fishing that often experienced poverty and hardship. He had opened a hospital in 1901 that became the headquarters of the Grenfell Mission.

While looking for support for his mission on a trip through New England, he met artist Jessie Luther. She had implemented craft-making as a form of therapy for folks recovering in sanitariums from chronic illness or nervous collapse. He immediately saw the positive effects of her work and invited her to join his project in the Canadian provinces of Newfoundland and Labrador.

Luther's plan was to introduce weaving as a means of producing salable goods from each person's home. She quickly found that implementing weaving would require not only teaching a new craft to locals but also importing the bulky and costly looms and getting them out to remote areas for use. Instead, she realized that rug hooking—using burlap sacks and scraps of old fabric—had long been a favorite practice of local women. Women enjoyed making hooked mats so much that the slow fishing months of February and March were known as "matting season" all along the coast.

Jessie Luther saw the potential in teaching women to refine their craft while developing a market for their wares in cities to the south. They featured arctic animals, depictions of Indigenous and local people, and picturesque scenes of life in Newfoundland and Labrador.

Over the next decade Grenfell opened more hospitals and branches of the mission and started Grenfell Industrial, a company to help folks

Rug made from silk stockings showing a small-town scene with a team of huskies pulling a sled, circa 1916

achieve better financial stability by creating an international market for the hooked mats. Luther was succeeded in her work by a series of women who strove to lead the women of the Grenfell Industrial to greater and greater success. By the 1920s, the mats and other homewares were being sold all over North America, creating a steady stream of support income for families that had often been on the edge of extreme poverty.

As their industry developed, one of their biggest needs was fabric for rug making. They received some donations, but in the era before fast fashion, most fabric was used and reused until it was worn to rags. Then in 1926, a Scotswoman named Mae Alice Pressley-Smith joined the Grenfell Mission. She had the idea to solicit used silk stockings as a new hooking material for the rugs. Silk rugs would be softer and more luxurious, and stockings were daily thrown away by the thousands. Women everywhere wore silk, and later rayon, stockings every day, and while they could be mended a little, they were easily destroyed by too many runs and snags. Yet no matter how worn, they could be dyed beautiful colors and hooked into rugs of every design.

In the mid-1920s, Grenfell Mission began soliciting donations of used silk stockings from Canada, the United States, and the United Kingdom with the slogan "When your stockings run, let them run to Labrador." In a letter to the Episcopal Academy of Philadelphia asking for more stockings, Dr. Grenfell wrote, "If you and your friends can help us this way, you would really be giving a 'leg-up' to Labrador." He even asked for, and received, used stockings from the dancers of the Folies Bèrgere in Paris. In 1929, nine tons of silk and rayon stockings and undergarments were received from all over the world. Because of these developments, the Grenfell Mission provided a lucrative and satisfying home-based occupation to folks up and down the coast that endured during the Depression. Sadly, fabric shortages during World War II and changes in import laws between the United States and Canada brought the silk-stocking mat industry to a close in the early 1940s. But the artistry of the families of rug hookers can still be seen in these gorgeous mats that still exist in homes and antique stores today.

Wearable Art

2.4

In this section of the book, we delve into the world of clothing and accessories. It might sound unusual, but tufting can be used to create or accent an array of beautiful and functional wearable pieces. The resulting items are not only stunning but also provide an added dimension of texture and depth.

When adding tufting to your wardrobe you can use a range of materials, including wool, cotton, and silk, allowing for endless possibilities in terms of texture, color, and pattern. Tufting can also be used in combination with other techniques, such as embroidery or beading, to create even more intricate and dynamic pieces.

opposite: Juanita Salazar, *Wild Wild Vest*, vest and hat, tufted and sewn acrylic, canvas, and felt

Melissa Monroe

Portland, Oregon

Melissa Monroe is an unstoppable creative force! A self-taught painter, sculptor, videographer, and musician, she added tufting to her repertoire in 2020. Her work radiates intense emotion, from the joy of her playful tufted purses and masks to the eerie melancholy of her performances and videos. By embracing flaws and abnormalities in her process, she creates a unique visual language that's equal parts bizarre and intimate.

Monroe describes her work as silly-serious, suggestive of her childhood in the 1980s and '90s. Her art uses imagery that makes her laugh and cry while exposing the joys and pains of growing up. Her tufted masks were inspired by 1920s amusement masks she saw in an oddities shop. They evoke the spiritual practice of play and the way we try on identities when we are young. By making and wearing these masks, Monroe connects with her younger self and discovers new facets of her personality.

Passion for the creative process, not just the outcome, is critical. As for Monroe's plans, she's eager to continue exploring her artistic journey and finding new ways to unleash her boundless creativity.

above
Melissa Monroe, *Face Hider* and other pieces (in progress), wool and vintage fabric hand tufted and sewn

right
Melissa Monroe, *Face Hider*, wool and vintage fabric hand tufted and sewn

SHAWL COLLAR

A big collar is a great way to add flare to a new jacket or a secondhand find. This project will attach a bright shaggy collar to a corduroy jacket but could also be used on a larger winter coat or a heavy overshirt. While it is possible to create whole garments from tufting, if you are not an experienced sewer you can use the structure of an existing garment as a canvas for your creativity.

You can trace the exact measurements of the collar from the garment you will be adding this to. This is perfect for items with distinctive features like huge lapels or patch pockets where you want tufted pieces that closely match the shape of your garment. A different method, and the one we are doing, is to use a collar pattern from another jacket and copy those dimensions from that piece. We found an existing jacket with a shawl collar in a thrift store that works perfectly; it gives a lot of space to tuft and looks good on almost any coat. You can find shawl collar patterns that might work for your piece online as well.

This project and the next were tufted together on the large frame we built in the second chapter (see page 41). When using the larger frame, it makes sense to use as much of the space as possible, to avoid wasting fabric.

– – – –

FINISHED SIZE: 29 × 22 inches (73.7 × 56 cm)

FOR THE PATTERN:

Pattern paper or craft paper

Jacket

Sewing pattern tracing wheel

Scissors

Pencil

FOR THE TUFTED DESIGN:

Tufting frame (approximately 72 × 68 inches/183 × 172.7 cm) with weights

Tufting cloth (36 × 36 inches/ 91.4 × 91.4 cm)

Masking tape

Ruler or compass

Sharpie markers

Threader

3 to 4 pounds (1.3 to 1.8 kg) yarn in two colors

Cut-pile, Duo, or AK-III tufting machine

Scissors or thread snips

FOR FINISHING:

Latex mask-making glue or flexible fabric glue

Spreader or paint roller

Face mask

Roberts 8200 contact adhesive

Felt backing cloth

Long dressmaker or sewing pins

Needle and thread

Thimble

For the pattern:
Roll out the pattern paper or craft paper, then lay your jacket, coat, or thrifted collar on top of it as flat as you can get it.

—

Using the tracing wheel, carefully follow around the outer edges of the collar and then firmly across the seam of the jacket in order to transfer the shape to the paper underneath.

—

Cut out your pattern piece along the indented lines. Since the collar is symmetrical, you can check the shape by folding it in half. [**FIG.1**]

For the tufted design:
Set up your frame and stretch your fabric (see page 64). Use the masking tape to cover the area of carpet tack near the yarn feeder to prevent yarn snags, as shown on page 76.

—

Transfer your collar pattern directly onto the tufting cloth using a pencil. Use a ruler or a compass to draw a 2-inch (5 cm) border around the edges.

—

Thread your machine, following the directions on page 77.

—

This project uses two strongly contrasting colors to create a very graphic effect. To make the details stand out you can start by tufting the droplets and drip lines.

—

If your design is going to be symmetrical, go back and forth while making the drops to keep everything lined up.

—

Once the details are in place, fill in the rest of the drip color around the back of the collar.

—

Change to the second color and fill in the remainder of the design. Keep checking for symmetry as you go. Try not to go over the edge of the pattern when you tuft. It's essential to be as accurate as possible so your final pieces will fit your garment correctly. [**FIG. 2**]

—

Trim any long threads on the front and back for a clean finish.

1

Top left: Design tests for tufted drips;
top middle: Pocket patches for skirt
(see page 164); top right: Shawl collar;
bottom: Skirt band

For finishing:

Glue the back of the piece while it is still stretched on the frame. Apply the glue evenly across the threads with a spreader or roller, getting some glue onto every strand. If you use latex glue (the most flexible option), the smell can be quite bad. Use in a well-ventilated area and wear a face mask when applying. If you are using rug glue, water it down to reduce the stiffness.

—

Once the piece is glued and dried, cut it off the frame. When making a tufted piece that you are going to sew, you don't want to glue down the edges of the tufting cloth since it's very hard to sew through the glue. Instead, you will roll the edge of tufting cloth under while you are sewing it.

—

We're attaching the collar at the neck edge so that it can stand up or lay down as you like. Because of this, the back side of the collar may be visible, so we are taking the extra step to back our tufted piece with fabric. [**FIG. 3**]

—

Set up a space to work outside and wear a face mask to avoid breathing in any mist.

—

Mask off the edges so the glue doesn't get on the yarn sticking out. Spray contact adhesive onto the backs of the collar and the backing cloth.

—

Let them become a little tacky, then lay the backing cloth onto the collar. Once they are put together, they will be difficult to reposition, so make sure the collar and backing match up. Smooth the backing out from the center and let the glue dry. Trim away the excess to leave a clean edge.

—

Once the backing cloth has been glued and dried, sew your collar piece onto the jacket. Lay the tufting onto the jacket and pin it in place to keep things aligned as you stitch them together.

—

Begin hand sewing the collar to the jacket using a running stitch or whipstitch. Once it's in place, you have a unique and cozy customized jacket.
[**FIGS. 4-5**]

SKIRT BAND

One of the disadvantages of wearing tufted fabric is that it can be stiff and heavy. This project uses those aspects to our advantage by adding a wide band to the bottom of an A-line skirt. The stiffness of the band helps the skirt stand away from the body in a style reminiscent of poodle skirts from the 1950s. This would also look great on a maxi dress or the bottom of a duster.

For this project, we'll be adding a 6-inch (15.2 cm) tufted border to the bottom of a sweet skirt. We decided to add pocket accents to tie it together a little.

– – – –

FINISHED SIZE: 136 × 6 inches (345.4 × 15.2 cm)

FOR THE PATTERN:

Pattern paper or craft paper

Skirt or dress

Long dressmaker or sewing pins

Tracing wheel

Scissors

FOR THE TUFTED DESIGN:

Tufting frame (approximately
    72 × 68 inches/183 × 172.7 cm)
    with weights

Tufting cloth (78 × 72 inches/
    198.1 × 183 cm)

Masking tape

Straightedge or ruler

Sharpie markers

Threader

Loop, cut-pile, Duo, or AK-III
    tufting machine

3 to 4 pounds (1.3 to 1.8 kg)
    yarn in three colors

Scissors or thread snips

FOR FINISHING:

Latex mask-making glue or
    flexible fabric glue

Spreader or paint roller

Needle and thread

Thimble

For the pattern:

Roll out the pattern paper or craft paper, then lay your skirt or dress bottom on top as flat as you can get it and pin it to the paper. A-line and circle skirts can be quite large when flattened out, so we'll be tracing half the skirt hem at a time and will tuft it twice.

—

Using the tracing wheel, carefully follow the bottom edge and side seams of the skirt or dress and trace firmly across the garment to transfer the shape to the paper underneath. A long point tracing wheel will pierce through the fabric to the paper underneath, leaving a dotted line of points that you can connect together in pen to make your pattern piece. This is not recommended for delicate fabrics or knits (but those wouldn't be a good choice for this project due to the weight of the tufted band). [**FIG.1**] Cut out the pattern.

—

Our skirt had decorative pocket flaps that seemed like an ideal place for a tufted accent (see left image on page 162). Other options include covering patch pockets or the waistband with tufting. We took a pattern of the pocket flaps using the tracing wheel and paper as described in the step above.

—

As mentioned, our skirt diameter was quite large, so we will be making it in two sections. If you are doing it this way, make sure to mirror one of the pieces in case the dress bottom isn't 100 percent symmetrical. [**FIG.2**]

—

Divide the skirt band into five sections and draw the dividing lines along the paper like stripes in a rainbow.

For the tufted design:

Set up your frame and stretch your fabric (see page 64). Use the masking tape to cover the area of carpet tack near the yarn feeder to prevent yarn snags, as shown on page 76.

—

Tape your pattern pieces to the back of your tufting cloth and trace the design. Then move the pattern pieces to another area on the frame and trace them again. Make sure to leave at least 2 inches (5 cm) between each piece so you will have enough space to cut each out with a border.

—

1

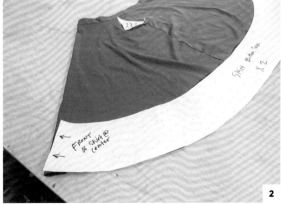

2

3

We wanted to make the most out of a three-color design, so we tufted this in a gradient of horizontal bands. It was tufted in loops with the AK-III with the lowest section using longer loops to create a fringe effect along the bottom of the skirt.

—

Set your machine to the lower pile height. Thread with two strands of cyan and tuft along the top edge of the design, following the curve. Tuft two or three more rows following the first until you have filled in the top section.

—

Tuft the pocket flaps with two threads of cyan at the same pile height as the skirt band.

—

Tuft the second section with one strand of cyan and one strand of royal blue. The third will use two strands of royal blue and the fourth will use one strand of royal blue and one of forest green. Each of these sections are tufted at the same pile height as the first.

—

For the last section, adjust your pile height to a higher setting and thread your machine with two strands of forest green. Fill in the last section.

—

Trim any loops on the front that are overly long and clean up the extra threads on the back.

For finishing:

Glue the back of the piece while it is still stretched on the frame. Apply the glue thinly and evenly across the threads with a spreader or roller, getting some glue onto every strand.

—

Once it is glued and dried, you can cut your tufted pieces off the frame, leaving 1 to 2 inches (2 to 5 cm) all around to tuck under. Don't glue the extra fabric down as you have on earlier projects since it is very difficult to sew through glue.

—

It's time to sew your tufted pieces onto the skirt or dress. Lay the tufting on the garment and pin together. This will help keep things aligned as you sew. [**FIG. 3**]

—

Trim the excess tufting cloth and sew the pieces together using a running stitch or whipstitch. Start by sewing the bottom edge of the tufted band to the bottom edge of the skirt or dress; this will keep the band perfectly aligned with the skirt. As you sew, try to keep the tufting cloth tucked under the tufting so it doesn't show. The sewing thread will disappear into the pile of the tufting, so perfect stitches are not important.

—

Repeat the process and attach the top of the skirt band to the skirt. Add the pocket accent pieces the same way.

—

If any of the tufting cloth shows around the top edge you can sew some loops to the skirt fabric with a tacking stitch to hide it. Cut off any loose threads and you are ready to wear it. [**FIG. 4**]

4

JEAN JACKET PATCHES

Blue jean jackets are a timeless wardrobe staple that provide an amazing canvas for personal expression. Their durable construction makes them perfect for applying large pieces of tufting without being pulled out of shape. They also have a long history of being customized by artists and fashionistas over the decades. While this project focuses on a large panel, you can also make patches of any size to add to the front or to a purse or backpack.

– – – –

FINISHED SIZE: 12 × 15 inches (30.5 × 38.1 cm)

FOR THE PATTERN:

Pattern paper or craft paper

Jacket

Long dressmaker or sewing pins

Sewing pattern tracing wheel

Pencil

Scissors

FOR THE TUFTED DESIGN:

Tufting frame (approximately
    30 × 30 inches/76.2 × 76.2 cm)
    with clamps

Tufting cloth (36 × 36 inches/
    91 × 91 cm)

Masking tape

Straightedge or ruler

Sharpie markers

Threader

3 to 4 pounds (1.3 to 1.8 kg)
    yarn in five colors

Cut-pile or Duo tufting machine

Scissors or thread snips

FOR FINISHING

Latex mask-making glue or
    flexible fabric glue

Spreader or paint roller

Needle and thread

Thimble

For the pattern:

Roll out the pattern paper or craft paper, then lay your jean jacket on top as flat as you can get it and pin the area of the jacket you want to trace to the paper.

—

Using the tracing wheel, carefully follow the back panel of the jacket, pressing through the garment to transfer the shape to the underlying paper. It may be hard to see the pinholes left by the tracing wheel. If so, you can trace over the holes with a pencil.

—

You can draw your design on the paper and transfer it to the tufting cloth. Designs like this with a lot of straight lines can be easier to draw flat on paper rather than trying to freehand them onto the stretched fabric. Cut out the paper pattern.

For the tufted design:

Set up your frame and stretch your fabric (see page 64). Use the masking tape to cover the area of carpet tack near the yarn feeder to prevent yarn snags, as shown on page 76.

—

Tape the paper pattern to the back of your tufting cloth, and trace the shape and your design onto the cloth.

—

Thread your machine, following the directions on page 77.

—

In a design like this you can start tufting anywhere. Pick a color and fill in all the areas that use that color. If you have decided to skip to this project first, refer back to the basic how to tuft steps on page 98. Otherwise, tuft your design in the outlined area using the techniques you have already mastered.

—

Trim any strands on the front that are overly long and clean up the extra threads on the back.

For finishing:

Glue the back of the piece while it is still stretched on the frame. Apply the glue thinly and evenly across the threads with a spreader or roller, getting some glue onto every strand.

—

Once the piece is glued and dried you can cut it off the frame, making sure to leave a small untufted edge. There's no need to glue down the edges of your finished piece for this project since you will use some of that border to sew the piece to your jacket.

—

Sew your tufted piece onto the jacket by carefully rolling the tufting fabric under and use a running or whipstitch. Admire your great handiwork and enjoy your new attire! [**FIG.1**]

Home Decor
2.5

This section features projects that integrate tufting into your home by adding it to three-dimensional objects and furnishings. These projects can be customized to your personal environment by varying the sizes or specifics. For example, you may want to adapt our chair cover instructions for a loveseat or make a slipcover for a smaller chair. Tufting is the perfect tool for creating maximalist home decor.

opposite: Venus Perez, *Frida Afterlife Glow*, wool, porcelain, and copper wire made with punch needle and sculpting tools

Selby Hurst Inglefield

London, United Kingdom

Selby Hurst Inglefield's tufted and sculptural art exudes a playful sophistication. Her upholstered furnishings seem like adult versions of a child's playhouse. This makes them at once nostalgic and contemporary, comforting and surprising.

Inglefield's ideas are mined from her personal writing and transformed through the therapeutic process of art making, turning something painful into something beautiful and poignant. Her tufted cat chairs were made after being in quarantine and becoming emotionally attached to the furniture in her home. The work is focused on feelings of appreciation and snugness in a time of loneliness and isolation. By combining her appreciation of household objects with her love of her cat companions, she has created objects of fantasy escapism grounded in her everyday environment.

top
Selby Hurst Inglefield, *Stripey Mog*, tufted wool on hessian and plastic chair

bottom
Selby Hurst Inglefield, *Troy's Blue Eyeshadow*, tufted wool on hessian and metal chair

STOOL SEAT COVER

Tufting is a fantastic material for upholstering objects in your living space. A simple place to start with covering furniture is a stool seat. Our friend made us a funky stool out of wood scraps so we could create a cover for it. But this technique will work on any footrest, bench, or barstool, adding a little extra padding to make hanging out more comfortable.

In this project, you will learn basic pattern making and upholstery work.

– – – –

FINISHED SIZE: 20 × 20 inches (50.8 × 50.8 cm)

FOR THE PATTERN:

Cardboard or thick paper

Stool

Pencil

Ruler or flexible tape measure

Compass (optional)

Scissors

FOR THE TUFTED DESIGN:

Tufting frame (approximately
  30 × 30 inches/76.2 × 76.2 cm)
  with clamps

Tufting cloth (36 × 36 inches/
  91.4 × 91.4 cm)

Masking tape

Sharpie markers

Threader

3 to 4 pounds (1 to 2 kg)
  yarn in seven colors

Tufting machine of choice

Scissors or thread snips

FOR FINISHING:

Mesh backing

Rug glue

Spreader or small paint roller

Upholstery foam

Long utility knife

Heavy-duty stapler or
  pneumatic upholstery
  stapler

For the pattern:

Start by creating a pattern for your stool top. Put a piece of cardboard or thick paper on your workbench. Place your stool or stool top face down on the cardboard or paper. Trace the outline of the stool onto the cardboard or paper.

—

Use a ruler or flexible tape measure to measure the thickness of the edge of the stool (in our case, it is ¾ inch/2 cm). [**FIG.1**]

—

Using a compass, if you have one, add the thickness of the stool top plus another 2 inches (5 cm) to create a border around the traced pattern (we added 2¾ inches/7 cm). You will need this extra width to wrap around any padding and to pull and staple the rug to the stool top. [**FIG.2**] Cut out the template.

For the tufted design:

Set up your frame and stretch your fabric (page 64). Use the masking tape to cover the area of carpet tack near the yarn feeder to prevent yarn snags, as shown on page 76.

—

Trace the template onto your stretched tufting cloth. We transferred this design by projecting it onto the stretched tufting cloth and tracing it with a marker.

—

Mark the colors you'd like to use onto your design.

—

In a design like this you can start tufting anywhere. Pick a color and fill in all the areas that use that color. If this is your first project from this book, you can refer back to the how to tuft steps on page 98. Otherwise, tuft your design in the outlined area using the techniques you have already mastered, with gusto.

—

Trim any strands on the front that are overly long and clean up the extra threads on the back.

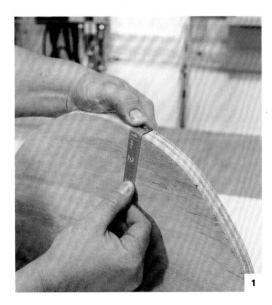

For finishing:

Use the template to cut out a piece of mesh backing the same size as your stool seat.

—

Glue the back of the piece while it is still stretched on the frame. Apply the glue evenly across the threads with a spreader or roller, getting some glue onto every strand.

—

Place the mesh backing against the back of the piece and use a spreader or roller to smooth the mesh into the wet glue.

—

Once the rug is glued and dried, you can cut your tufted piece off the frame. You don't need to glue down the edges of the tufting cloth; instead, cut your design and mesh backing out precisely at the edge of your tufting.

—

Use the pattern to cut a piece of upholstery foam. Beveling the top edge of the cushion makes it easier to cover without having to add any shaping. This can be done with a long utility knife. [**FIG. 3**]

—

It's time to upholster your stool. Lay your tufting face down on your workbench, table, or floor, set the foam upside down on it, then, finally, your stool. Center the stool so all sides of the tufting can reach the underside of the stool. You should have a 1- to 2-inch (2.5 to 5 cm) border of tufting to staple to the stool. [**FIG. 4**]

—

3

4

5

Begin stapling in a star pattern by starting in one spot, then moving to the opposite side. Repeat these steps at a right angle from the first two so you have four points stapled around the rim. This will ensure the tufting is stapled evenly. [**FIG. 5-6**]

—

Repeat the process of pulling the tufting over and stapling it until the piece is finished. Pull your stool up to a table, have a seat, and enjoy a cold drink as a reward for your handiwork!

6

Denja Harris, *Soft Chain*, acrylic, polyfill, and yarn waste, machine tufted using a cut-pile tufting machine

THROW PILLOW

This project takes you step-by-step through creating a unique pillow for your home. Get ready to add a pop of personality and comfort to your space with your handcrafted creation. Throw pillows add color, texture, and comfort to a room, instantly transforming the ambience. They can be used to complement existing decor or serve as the space's focal point. Whether you want to make a statement, create a cozy atmosphere, or add a touch of softness, a handmade throw pillow is a versatile and affordable way to enhance your home.

One issue with tufting pillows is keeping them flexible so they are comfortable to use. Many types of glue can dry to be very stiff–such as Elmer's or carpet glue, if applied too thickly. You can choose a standard throw pillow size or be creative with shapes and sizes. Using standard sizes makes it easy to find inserts, but any shape can be stuffed with cotton batting or polyfill. We collect all of our tufting scraps to use as filling.

– – – –

FINISHED SIZE: 22 × 22 inches (56 × 56 cm)

FOR THE PATTERN:

Cardboard or thick paper

Straightedge or ruler

Pencil

Scissors

FOR THE TUFTED DESIGN:

Tufting frame (approximately
30 × 30 inches/76.2 × 76.2 cm)
with clamps

Tufting cloth (36 × 36 inches/
91.4 × 91.4 cm)

Masking tape

Straightedge or ruler

Sharpie markers

Threader

3 to 4 pounds (1 to 2 kg) yarn
in six colors

Cut-pile or Duo tufting machine

Scissors or thread snips

FOR FINISHING:

Latex mask-making glue or
flexible fabric glue

Spreader or small paint roller

Sewing machine

Zipper

Fabric for back of pillow

Binder clips or dressmaker pins

Pillow insert, polyfill, or waste
yarn scraps

For the pattern:

Making a pattern for a throw pillow can be as easy as drawing a square if you already know what your dimensions are. I like to draw the pattern on cardboard or thick paper so I can keep it for future projects.

—

We are making a standard-size throw pillow, 22 × 22 inches (56 × 56 cm). This is a good size for couch cushions, and it is easy to find premade pillowcases and inserts of this size. Use a straight-edge and pencil to draw the pillow template, then cut it out.

For the tufting:

Set up your frame and stretch your fabric (see page 64). Use the masking tape to cover the area of carpet tack near the yarn feeder to prevent yarn snags, as shown on page 76. Hold the template against the stretched tufting cloth and trace around it. Draw your design onto the fabric or project an image and trace it inside the outline of the pillow.

—

Thread your machine, following the directions on page 77.

—

Pick a color and start filling in all the areas that use it. If this is the first project in this book that you are tufting you can refer back to the how to tuft steps on page 98. Otherwise, tuft your design in the outlined area using the techniques you already mastered, with verve. It can be fun to experiment with texture on pillows since it is so easy to run your hands over them. Trim any strands on the front that are overly long and clean up the extra threads on the back.

For the finishing:

Glue the back of the piece while it is still stretched on the frame. Apply the glue thinly and evenly across the threads with a spreader or roller, getting some glue onto every strand.

—

Once the piece is glued and dried, you can cut it off the frame. Leave a 1- to 2-inch (2.5 to 5 cm) fabric border around it for seam allowances.

—

For our pillow we decided to sew a backing with a zipper. If you have a sewing machine, you can find a number of tutorials online on how to sew a zippered pillow, but we're also including steps below.

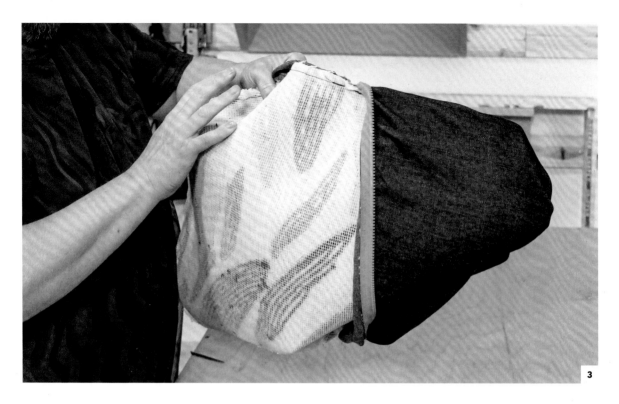

3

In this case, instead of fabric for the pillow front, you'll be using your tufting. After you sew the tufting to the pillow backing you'll need to turn it right side out—zippers make this part easier.

—

To sew a zipper pillow back you'll need a zipper larger than your pillow width as well as two pieces of fabric. For our pillow size, we need two pieces of fabric measuring 23 × 12 inches (58 × 30 cm).

—

Place the zipper face down onto the long side of one of the pieces of fabric so the width of the zipper is entirely on top of the fabric and sew along the edge.

—

Press the fabric away from the zipper and top stitch the fabric alongside the zipper teeth to achieve a clean edge. Repeat these steps for the other piece of fabric.

—

Now you have two pieces of fabric connected by a zipper in the middle that is the same size as your tufted pillow front.

—

Lay the back of your pillow face up and place your tufted piece face down on top of it. Make sure the zipper is not all the way closed. Carefully clip or pin your pillow back to your tufted piece face-to-face. The seam allowance should be about ½ inch (1.3 cm).

—

Start by sewing a few stitches at each of the four corners. Since the tufted piece and the backing fabric are so different, sewing them together can sometimes lead to the fabric pulling and your pillow looking a little wonky. Stitching down the corners first really helps the finished pillow look perfect. [**FIG.1**]

—

Guide the piece carefully through your sewing machine, trying to get as close to the edge of the tufting as possible. Most sewing machines (even industrial ones) will not sew through the glue on the tufted sections. We've found that using a narrow foot or zipper foot on your machine will allow you to get very close to the tufted edge. [**FIG. 2**]

—

After you have sewn all four sides, trim the excess fabric from all sides and the corners to remove bulk from the seams.

—

Unzip the zipper from the inside and turn your pillow right side out and stuff it with the filling of your choice. You can use a chopstick to push the filling tightly into the corners and seams so it looks nice and plump. [**FIG. 3**]

—

Admire your hard work. [**FIG. 4**]

4

CHAIR SLIPCOVER

This ambitious project will create a showstopper throne for your home. A custom slipcover can completely transform the look and feel of your furniture. It protects your chair from wear and tear and allows you to give it a new lease on life by changing its style and color. It also gives new life to a chair that has been stained or damaged but is still comfortable. So get tufting and say hello to a refreshed and rejuvenated piece that fits your style and enhances your decor!

In this project, we'll create a pattern piece using simple draping techniques on a chair. We will be tufting this in a super-high pile (about 2 inches/5 cm) to give a plush and luxurious feel, but low pile is also a great option.

If taking a pattern from an existing chair feels daunting, you can also find a premade slipcover and design your tufted piece to those specs. Once each section is tufted, glued, and backed, we'll show how to sew it into the final cover, and your entirely tufted armchair will become the coziest statement piece in the house.

For this project, use flexible glue so the finished piece can drape over the chair and is comfortable to sit on. We recommend using either flexible fabric glue or mask-making latex.

_ _ _ _

FINISHED SIZE: 84 × 72 inches (213.4 × 183 cm)

FOR THE PATTERN:
Chair
3 to 5 yards (2.5 to 3 m)
    muslin or thin woven cloth
Long dressmaker or sewing pins
Scissors
Laser level or ruler
Marker or pencils
Large sheet of paper (pattern
    drafting paper is available at
    most sewing stores)

FOR THE TUFTED DESIGN:
Tufting frame (approximately
    96 × 96 inches/244 × 244 cm)
    with weights
Tufting cloth (104 × 104 inches/
    264 × 264 cm)
Masking tape
Straightedge or ruler
Sharpie markers
Compass or ruler
Threader
30 to 40 pounds (14 to 18 kg) yarn
Cut-pile, Duo, or AK-III tufting
    machine
Scissors or thread snips

FOR FINISHING:
Latex mask-making glue or
    flexible fabric glue
Spreader or small paint roller
Bulldog clips
Large needle (upholstery or leather)
Yarn or thick upholstery thread

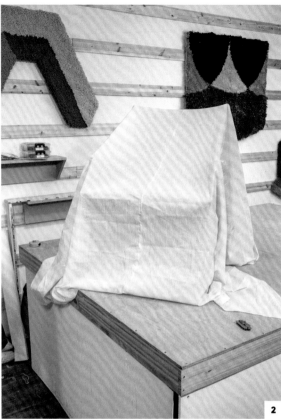

For the pattern:

Find a chair you'd like to create a tufted slipcover for. We've chosen one with a simple shape, so the cover can slip on easily. [**FIG.1**]

—

Using a large piece of muslin, cover the chair loosely. The fabric will drape in a natural way around the corners of the chair. Tuck the cloth in the cracks of the seat cover, so the fabric matches the form of the chair more closely. [**FIG.2**]

—

Moving around the chair, pinch the excess cloth in your hand and pin it into a fold close to the chair. Doing this will begin to reveal the chair form with the cloth. [**FIG.3**]

—

After doing this over the entire piece, you can now cut away the excess fabric that won't be used. This will produce a template that resembles the shape of the chair. [**FIG.4**]

—

Make adjustments to the pins, if necessary.

—

Straighten the bottom fabric—the fabric closest to the floor—by either using a laser level or measuring from the bottom of the chair legs upward. This will give you a clean finish at the bottom. [**FIG.5**]

—

Make notes on the cloth with a marker or pencil indicating what section of the chair it is (front, right side, and so forth). It should be self-explanatory but notes always help.

—

Remove the fabric cover from the chair, unpin it, and lay it flat. You will have an abstract-looking fabric.

—

Lay the paper underneath the fabric so you can trace the fabric pattern onto it. Paper will be easier to transfer to your tufting frame. Paper of this size can be found on rolls at art supply stores.

—

Cut out the pattern piece.

—

If the paper doesn't fit on the tufting cloth, you will need to cut your chair cover into separate pieces and tuft them individually. (We tufted our slipcover as a single piece.) You can also cut the paper piece apart to fit on the frame more efficiently. If you need to do this, note where the pieces attach to one another.

—

6

For the tufted design:

Set up your frame and stretch your fabric (see page 64). Use the masking tape to cover the area of carpet tack near the yarn feeder to prevent yarn snags, as shown on page 76. Hold the template against the stretched tufting cloth and trace around it using a straightedge and ruler.

—

Add a ½-inch (1.3 cm) border or seam allowance around the perimeter. The easiest way to do this is by going around the pattern piece with a compass set to ½ inch (1.3 cm).

—

Draw or transfer your design onto the pattern piece(s) on the frame. In our case, we designed the pattern on the computer and projected it onto the tufting cloth.

—

Thread your machine following the directions on page 77.

—

If this is the first project you are tufting, I admire your courage! But be sure to review the how to tuft steps on page 98.

—

Tuft your design staying within the pattern piece without tufting into the seam allowance border. [**FIG. 6**]

—

Trim any strands on the front that are overly long and clean up the extra threads on the back.

For finishing:

Glue the back of the piece(s) while still stretched on the frame. Apply the glue thinly and evenly across the threads with a spreader or roller, getting some glue onto every strand. Use flexible glue so the finished piece can drape over the chair and is comfortable to sit on. We recommend using either flexible fabric glue or mask-making latex. Do not glue into the seam allowance border, so sewing is easier.

—

After the glue dries, cut out the panel(s) from the frame. [**FIG.7**] Begin laying them on the chair.

—

Using bulldog clips, roughly clip the edges together and confirm they're a good fit. Remove the clips.

—

Now turn over your tufted piece(s) with the tufting facing the chair.

—

Using the bulldog clips, clip together the edges again. This will reveal the seam allowance so you can easily hand stitch the seams together. [**FIG.8**]

—

Using a large needle, stitch together the slipcover. For thread, we used the same wool yarn with which we tufted the piece, which provides sufficient strength to hold the seams together and made stitching relatively easy. A simple running stitch or whipstitch will do.

—

7

Continue this process until the slipcover is completely stitched together. [**FIG. 9**]

—

Sew or glue the bottom edge to leave a clean finish.

—

Remove the slipcover from the chair, turn it inside out, and put it back on your chair. [**FIG. 10**]

8

9

10

Qualeasha Wood

Brooklyn, New York

Qualeasha Wood is a celebrated contemporary artist who makes tufted work as well as woven tapestries. Her love of queer craft and family ties to textile work inspired her to work in this medium.

Wood often uses technological iconography with self-referential portraiture to discuss how Black femme figures are invaluable to culture while simultaneously objectified and held at the margins. She is intentional about her work, often with her portraits making direct eye contact with the viewer to deliver this message.

Wood's work comes from a place of advocacy for inclusivity in the arts. She has spoken openly about being left out of museums and institutions because, as a young Black woman, she never saw herself represented in those spaces. Because of this, she feels strongly that her work should make the younger version of herself and all the young girls out there feel seen and understood.

top
Qualeasha Wood, *Circle the Drain*, machine-tufted acrylic

bottom
Qualeasha Wood, *Beneath the Garden*, machine-tufted acrylic

CAT TOWER

Banish the boring beige cat tower forever by creating a multilevel maximalist habitat for your feline overlord. This project will show you how to re-cover an existing cat tower or cover one of your own design. Once you understand the basics of taking a pattern from an object, you can cover almost any shape with tufting (although some shapes are easier than others). We are working from a cat tower we previously made from scratch, but it is also possible to re-cover one that has gotten a little too shredded.

Since this is such an ambitious project, we'll be using the large frame we built on page 41. This way you can draw all your pattern pieces on one frame and tuft it all together.

FOR THE PATTERN:

Cat tower (can be new, used, or one you've created)
Flexible ruler or tape measure
Marker or pencil
Cardboard or thick paper
Scissors

FOR THE TUFTED DESIGN:

Tufting frame (approximately 72 × 68 inches/183 × 172.7 cm) with weights
Tufting cloth (78 × 72 inches/ 198.1 × 183 cm)
Masking tape
Straightedge or ruler
Sharpie markers
Threader
12 to 16 pounds (5.5 to 7 kg) yarn
Tufting machine of choice
Scissors or thread snips

FOR FINISHING:

Rug glue
Spreader or small paint roller
Heavy-duty stapler or pneumatic upholstery stapler

For the pattern:

When starting with a premade cat tower, it can be helpful to take it apart so you can make simple pattern pieces from it. For example, most cat trees have central posts that would be great to cover with tufting. If your cat tower is disassembled, lay each part of the tree that you want to cover on a piece of paper and trace the shape. Make sure to label each pattern piece.

—

In this case, instead of taking it apart, we are taking measurements of the surfaces that we want to cover. We chose flat surfaces that were easy to measure and created paper pattern pieces for each section we wanted to cover in tufted panels. [**FIG.1**] Carefully measure each section and transfer to your cardboard or thick paper. [**FIG.2**]

—

Decide if you want the tufting to go over the edges, like we did on the stool seat (page 173), or if you want to attach it to the wood surface, as we did in

3

the picture frame/mirror project (page 127). If you want to go around the surfaces to the other side, measure and add enough extra space to the pattern pieces to cover the edges plus an extra 2 inches (5 cm).

—

Cut out the pattern pieces.

For the tufted design:

Set up your frame and stretch your fabric (see page 64). Use the masking tape to cover the area of carpet tack near the yarn feeder to prevent yarn snags, as shown on page 76. Hold the template against the stretched tufting cloth and trace around it using a straightedge and marker. Leave 2 to 3 inches (5 to 7.6 cm) in between each pattern piece.

—

Transfer your design that will be tufted onto each pattern piece. In our case, we designed the pattern on the computer and projected it onto the cloth.

—

Thread your machine, following the directions on page 77.

—

If this is the first project you are tufting, I am in awe. But take a moment to review the how to tuft steps on page 98.

—

Tuft your design inside the outlined pattern pieces while your cat asks for more food. If you make a mistake and go over the line, be sure to pull out the excess to your tufted area so it perfectly matches the pattern piece.

—

Trim any loops on the front that are overly long and clean up the extra threads on the back.

For finishing:

Glue the backs of the pieces while still stretched on the frame. Apply the rug glue evenly across the threads with a spreader or roller, getting some glue onto every strand.

—

Once the rug is glued and dried, you can cut it off the frame.

—

Carefully match each pattern piece to the corresponding area on the cat tower.

—

Tuck the edge of the cloth under and staple to the wooden structure. It's best to staple between colors and spread the tufting apart so the staple won't be detected. [**FIGS. 3-5**]

—

Entice your cat up onto the tower with treats and catnip and enjoy your new TikTok following!

4

GLOSSARY

AIR SCRUBBER: An air purification device that removes particulate matter from the air by cycling the air through several layers of air filters. Its primary function is to make air breathable after it has been contaminated with dust or fumes. When tufting cut pile or applying glue, we recommend running an air scrubber so you aren't inhaling harmful yarn fibers and glue toxins.

CARPET TACK STRIP: Narrow lengths of wood that are used to keep wall-to-wall carpeting (or tufting cloth) in place. They're studded with hundreds of nails and are installed along the perimeter of the walls, tack side up. The nails are angled in one direction to grab the carpet (or tufting cloth) to hold it tight.

CONTACT ADHESIVE: Glue that is formulated to create a permanent bond when it sticks to itself. It is used by applying the glue to both working surfaces and left to get tacky. Once it is tacky, the two surfaces can be stuck to each other, creating a very strong bond. Often used to apply final backing to tufted rugs.

ELECTRIC CARVING CLIPPERS: Often used to shave human or animal hair, they are also perfect for carving into carpets to create separation between colors and enhance your design.

ELECTRIC CARVING SCISSORS: Electric scissors are used to bevel and carve carpets. They look like scissors in the front and can operate very fast to create sharp, clean lines in your tufted piece.

FELT BACKING: A nonwoven fabric material often made of recycled polyester. It comes in a variety of thicknesses and colors. Since it is nonwoven it won't fray at the edges when it's cut, so it works well when hand-finishing tufted rugs.

FORSTNER BIT: A kind of drill bit that bores precise flat-bottomed holes in wood, in any orientation with respect to the grain. It creates a much cleaner hole than a regular drill bit.

FRENCH CLEAT: A French cleat is a way of securing a cabinet, mirror, artwork, or other object to a wall. Several styles are readily available in metal or wood. It's easy to make on your own with a table saw by cutting a piece of lumber down the middle at a 45-degree angle. The two parts create a perfect match and so create a strong connection.

MESH BACKING: A leno-weave mesh backing made of an all-synthetic secondary backing fabric. It adds to the dimensional stability of the carpet, covers glued yarn ends, and gives your rug a more finished look without having to add a final backing. This is often applied to the rug at the same time as the glue is applied to create a permanent bond.

NONSKID BACKING: Felt backing with a rubber coating or dots that will keep your rug from sliding on the floor.

PNEUMATIC UPHOLSTERY STAPLER: Similar to a handheld staple gun but uses compressed air to operate. They are small in size, so easily fit in tight spaces.

ROVING: Wool that has not been spun or twisted, so it pulls apart very easily and probably won't work for tufting, even if you have the right thickness.

RUG GLUE: A specially formulated adhesive for locking in the tufts of your rug. It often contains latex or synthetic latex to offer flexibility and security so the tufts can't be pulled out of the backing.

SERGE BINDING: A faster alternative to sewing a whipstitch, created by using a serging machine. Although expensive, many rug and carpet repair businesses will do this work for very reasonable prices.

SHEEP SHEARS (WITH GUIDE): An electric clipper with a large comb at the front that is typically used to remove wool from a sheep. It's great for trimming and shaving carpets. Paired with a shearing guide, it can plane very fine layers off the top off a tufted rug to create a clean, flat surface.

SPREADER: A flat piece of plastic, wood, or metal used to spread rug glue on a tufted piece.

THREAD CLIPS: Small scissors that hang from your third finger as you sew, leaving the rest of your hand free to manage the needle and thread. They work great for tufting.

THREADER: A small metal wire or paper clip used to thread your tufting machine.

TUFTING MACHINE: A machine that punches yarn through a backing cloth to create a rug. They can be divided into five different types:
Handheld manual: These operate with the user's arm movement. Primarily used where electricity isn't readily available. Patents date back to the late 1850s.

Handheld electric-driven (the focus of this book): Invented in the late 1960s, they come in low- and high-pile versions. They can create a variety of carpet pile heights, from $\frac{1}{5}$ to $\frac{3}{4}$ inch (5 to 19 mm). Models include the AK-I, NK-II, AK-II, NK-I, ZQ-II, and KRD. Electric/pneumatic models can tuft carpet pile up to $2\frac{3}{4}$ inches (70 mm). Examples include the AK-III, ZQ-III, and Hofmann VML-16.
Sewing machine type: With up to twelve needles, this was invented in the late 1930s and used primarily to make bath mats and throw pillows. The tufts lock into the backing cloth without adhesive.
Broadloom type: Massive industrial machines with thousands of needles that create wall-to-wall carpets. These machines tuft dozens of rows at a time up to 15 feet (4.5 m) wide.
CNC type: Designs are created in a carpet design software, then uploaded to a computer, which gives the tufting head instructions for the path it is supposed to take. The computer alerts the user when yarn changes need to happen and if there are any tufting errors.

TWILL TAPE BINDING: A method of closing the edge of a rug by feeding twill tape into an industrial carpet sewing machine. Many rug and carpet businesses will sew twill tape on hand-tufted pieces for a low cost.

WHIPSTITCH: A type of sewing stitch in which the needle is passed in and out of the edge of a rug to create a series of circles. When yarn is used, it can create a clean finish for your rug by completely closing the edge off.

WOVEN BACKING: Woven fabric used for backing carpets and rugs. Generally sold in darker colors so it won't show dirt when placed on the floor.

opposite
Trish Andersen, *Highs and Lows*,
machine-tufted yarn

BIBLIOGRAPHY

The Carpet and Rug Institute. "History of Carpet." July 8, 2022, carpet-rug.org/about-us/history-of-carpet.

Clasper-Torch, Micah. "The History of Punch Needle." sisterMAG, May 27, 2021, www.sister-mag.com/en/magazine/sistermag-no-61-may-2021/the-history-of-punch-needle.

Deaton, Thomas M. *Bedspreads to Broadloom: The Story of the Tufted Carpet Industry*. Acton, MA: Color Wheel, 1993.

Huenemann, Karyn. "Mary B. Huber." *Canada's Early Women Writers*, January 22, 2013, ceww.wordpress.com/2013/01/22/mary-b-huber.

Insigné Carpets. "The History of Carpet." May 22, 2020, www.insignecarpets.com/blog/all/the-history-of-carpet.

Kit Kemp's Design Thread. "A True Collaboration—Alexander Calder." April 16, 2021, kitkemp.com/a-true-collaboration-alexander-calder.

Laverty, Paula. *Silk Stocking Mats: Hooked Mats of the Grenfell Mission*. Montreal: McGill-Queen's University Press, 2005.

Mathes, Charles. "All Calder Tapestries Are Not Created Equal." *Value & Thought*, August 15, 2015, www.valuethoughts.com/2015/04/30/all-calder-tapestries-are-not-created-equal.

Traditional Fine Arts Organization. "The Great American Cover Up: American Rugs on Beds, Tables, and Floors." September 9, 2007, tfaoi.org/aa/7aa/7aa797.htm.

von Rosenstiehl, Helene. *American Rugs and Carpets: From the Seventeenth Century to Modern Times*. London: Barrie & Jenkins, 1978.

Walsh, A. "Hand-Made in Guatemala, Custom-Made in France." *Financial Times*, September 28, 2012, www.ft.com/content/b9917416-07f3-11e2-a2d8-00144feabdc0.

Whitlock, Jan, and Tracy Jamar. *American Sewn Rugs: Their History with Exceptional Examples*. Self-published, 2012.

ACKNOWLEDGMENTS

It's almost impossible to give an account of all the support we received making this book, but we'll do our best. Sharing knowledge is one of the most important drivers for us as makers, and we are deeply grateful to everyone who has shared their skills and knowledge with us.

First and foremost, we would like to thank our editor, Holly La Due, who tirelessly worked with us through every draft, providing invaluable guidance and thought-provoking advice. In addition to Holly, the team at Princeton Architectural Press was instrumental in the production of the book. Managing editor Sara Stemen, design director Paul Wagner, designer Natalie Snodgrass, digital production coordinator Valerie Kamen, and publisher Lynn Grady deserve all the thanks in the world for their immense contributions.

Back before there was anything to design or edit, the first person who believed this could be a book was our encouraging agent, Soumeya Roberts at HG Literary. She helped us pull our scattered ideas into a proposal, introduced us to Holly, and guided us into the publishing world with great support. Hannah Popal provided positive and timely support from HG Literary as well.

While we were writing and developing the projects for the book, the small but mighty team of folks at Tuft the World kept everything going, with special thanks to Joe DiGiuseppe, Jenn McTague, Chrissy Scolaro, and Matthew Stiles. In addition to tufting and prepping projects, the team stepped in time and time again when we weren't as present at our company as we would have liked to be.

We'd like to thank all the tufting experts who have shared their knowledge with us and with the tufting community. All of the artists who participated in this book deserve so much credit for amazing artistry and for participating in this project. We feel so privileged to be able to share their work here.

And we must acknowledge the endless love and encouragement of our friends and family, without whom this book could never have been written.

As you find errors or issues in this book, please know that those mistakes were entirely our own and not the fault of anyone else who worked on this project.

Finally, we'd also like to thank everyone who has taken the time to read this book and for the feedback they have provided us. We sincerely hope that this book will help make tufting more accessible and open up a world of possibilities for the craft.

BOOK PRODUCTION TEAM

Jaime Alvarez: Photographer. Dozens of hours of photography, lighting, photo editing, and directing shoots. jaimephoto.com | *Alesandra Bevilacqua:* Book model | *Veronica Cianfrano:* Head tufter and designer of the carving project. The most fabulous crusher of all time and accidental book model | *Kate Garman:* Head tufter on hall runner project and book model | *Derek Hall:* Head tufter and designer of the carved name rug; head tufter of the cat tree project, the jacket collar, and the armchair slipcover; and book model | *Heather Holiday:* Photo stylist, videographer, and shoot assistant extraordinaire | *Camilla Martineli:* Photography assistant | *Vivien Wise:* Designer and tufter of the jean jacket patches and book model | *Zach Zecha:* Designer and maker of the wooden stool | *Clothing:* Lobo Mau, lobomau.com; Norblack Norwhite, norblacknorwhite.com | *Aprons:* Dusen Dusen, dusendusen.com; Blue Skies Workroom, blueskiesworkroom.com

WE'VE LEARNED SO MUCH FROM THESE PROFESSIONALS:

Scott Group Studio, scottgroupstudio.com
Kramis Teppich Design, kramis-teppich.ch

IMAGE CREDITS

All images were taken by Jaime Alvarez unless otherwise noted below.

Cover, 156: Ella Piecoup and Juanita Salazar
4: Sophie Bolton
5: Flavia Catena Photography
6, 7, 8: Molly Brennan
14, 21: Bequest of Henry Francis du Pont, Courtesy of the Winterthur Museum, Garden & Library
22, 23, 117 top: Chia Chong
49 top: Courtesy of the Bandy Heritage Center for Northwest Georgia
49 bottom, 67 top: Tim Eads
56: Courtesy of the Winterthur Museum, Garden & Library
63, 89: Aliyah Salmon
66: Cheekylorns—stock.adobe.com
71, 170: Venus Perez
72: Bequest of Elizabeth R. Vaughan, 2012, Art Institute of Chicago
73, 111 right, 200, 201: Lala touffe, aka Cléa Delogu
91 top: Courtesy of the Library of Congress
91 bottom left: Courtesy of the Biodiversity Library
91 bottom right: Courtesy of the Hagley Museum and Library
94, 103, 104, 105: Felicia Murray
96 top and bottom, 178: Department
106, 172: Selby Hurst Inglefield

117 bottom: Savannah College of Art and Design
124, 158, 202: Melissa Monroe
126: Andie Solar
132: Rebecca Coll
134: AJ Peterson
154: Gift of J. P. Stanley, courtesy of the Textile Museum of Canada
155 left: UK/Newfoundland Post Office, 1941
155 right: Courtesy of the Council for Canadian-American Relations/American Friends of Canada through the generosity of Mrs. Georgina M. Bissell and the Textile Museum of Canada
193 top and bottom: Ernst Fischer
205: Trish Andersen